Sadlier
Discovering God Program

A Faith-Development Program for

Five-Year-Olds

Discovering God's Love

Guide

by
Julie Brunet
and
Renée McAlister

Publisher
Gerard F. Baumbach, Ed.D.

Editor in Chief
Moya Gullage

Product Developer
Michaela Burke

William H. Sadlier, Inc.
9 Pine Street
New York, NY 10005–1002

is a registered trademark of William H. Sadlier, Inc.

Home Office:
9 Pine Street
New York, New York 10005–1002

ISBN:0-8215-2471-2
23456789/08 07 06 05 04

Nihil Obstat
Reverend John G. Stillmank, S.T.L.
Censor Librorum

Imprimatur
✠ Most Reverend William H. Bullock
Bishop of Madison
July 30, 1999

The *Nihil Obstat* and *Imprimatur* are official declarations that a book or pamphlet is free of doctrinal or moral error. No implication is contained therein that those who have granted the *Nihil Obstat* and *Imprimatur* agree with the contents, opinions, or statements expressed.

Acknowledgments
Original illustrations by Julie Brunet and Renée McAlister, recreated by Arthur Friedman

Editors: Joanna Dailey and Kathleen Hlavacek

Excerpts from the *New American Bible with Revised New Testament and Psalms* Copyright © 1991, 1986, 1970 Confraternity of Christian Doctrine, Inc., Washington, D.C. Used with permission. All rights reserved. No part of the *New American Bible* may be reproduced in any form without permission in writing from the copyright holder.

Excerpts from the *General Directory for Catechesis* Copyright © 1997 Libreria Editrice Vaticana—United States Catholic Conference, Inc. Used with permission. All rights reserved. The additional reference *DMC* refers to the *Directory of Masses with Children.*

Contents

Unit 3 Belonging to My Family

Catechist's Workshop

You Are A Catechist

Jesus came to bring the good news of God's love to the world. The Church is called to continue this mission—that means all of us, the members of the Church.

As a catechist to young children, you have been given the awesome responsibility of introducing them to God's love in an explicit way. Through your words, your active caring, and your leadership, you share the good news of Jesus' resurrection and his continued presence in each of our lives today. In these ways, you help each young child in your care to develop a personal relationship with God.

Preschool children are particularly open to this relationship, and the Church considers the catechesis of young children to be of utmost importance in laying a strong foundation of faith: "Infancy and childhood . . . are a time of primary socialization as well as of human and Christian education in the family, the school and the Church. These must then be understood as a decisive moment for subsequent stages of faith" (*General Directory for Catechesis*, 178).

Parents, of course, are the first catechists in a child's life. In their unique home setting, they provide the first community of faith for their child. Through their beliefs, values, and attitudes, parents lay the foundation of their child's knowledge and experience of the Christian life.

As a catechist to young children, you continue to build upon this foundation. While the Church affirms that "nothing replaces family catechesis," (*General Directory for Catechesis*,

178), the Church also affirms the catechetical process in infancy and early childhood. This process seeks to educate the child in every dimension: "It seeks to develop those human resources which provide an anthropological basis for the life of faith, a sense of trust, of freedom, of self-giving, of invocation and of joyful participation. Central aspects of the formation of children are training in prayer and introduction to Sacred Scripture" (*General Directory for Catechesis*, 178; *DMC,* 66).

The Discovering God Program seeks to introduce the preschool child to the Catholic community's life of faith in all these ways. While developing a child's human resources, it presents the faith in a language that the young child can understand. Presenting human life as a gift of God, the program engages the child's senses in incremental experiences of God, the gift of his Son, Jesus, the gifts of family, Catholic community, Scripture, sacraments, and prayer.

As a catechist to young children, your goals can be summarized in four words: *information, formation, instruction, participation.* You share information about the life of faith with the child through age-appropriate explanations and activities. Through simple prayer activities, you are involved in the formation of the young child's relationship with God. Through the introduction to Scripture, sacramental rituals, and other Catholic practices, you continue the instruction of the young child in the Catholic faith. All of this leads to the "joyful participation" in the life of faith noted in the *General Directory for Catechesis*. Through your care and concern for the little flock entrusted to you, you help to proclaim the good news Jesus Christ himself proclaimed to little ones: "Let the children come to me, and do not prevent them; for the kingdom of heaven belongs to such as these" (Matthew 19:14).

Catechetical Environment

Building Community

The family is the young child's first community of faith. When you as catechist introduce the child into a larger community of faith, you build upon this basic familial faith and love. However, you add an important dimension of relationship in faith, that of baptismal oneness in Christ. In recognizing and accepting each child as a child of God, you prepare the child to know and love God—Father, Son, and Spirit—in a personal life of faith.

You recognize and accept each child as a child of God when you:

- welcome each child to the group and call each by name
- ensure that each child feels accepted and safe
- love and care for each child as an individual
- treat each child with dignity and respect, showing no favoritism
- show enthusiasm during the time you spend with each child
- share your personal experiences with the children, encouraging them to do the same.

Group Atmosphere

Young children learn best in a group atmosphere that is open, friendly, inviting, and secure. You can encourage such an atmosphere in your group by taking the lead in praise and encouragement. Young children need words directly addressed to them. When praising your group for good work, always saying "Good job, everyone!" is not sufficient. Try to praise individuals by name whenever possible. "I saw you hang your coat in your cubby, Stacy. That was great." The youngest children may need your help in verbalizing their feelings and desires. A child grabbing a toy may need to hear you say, "Do you want that toy? You can ask, 'May I have a turn?'"

A catechist for preschool children is:

- a rich and constant source of praise and encouragement
- respectful of a young child's need to share and need to play or work independently
- a celebrator of special events in the lives of the group members (such as birthdays)
- a focus of cooperation in group activities, helping the children to help one another
- a non-judgmental listener to all, so that children can express thoughts and feelings without being afraid.

Physical Setting

Young children learn best when they are free to explore their surroundings through active play. An ideal preschool environment provides opportunities for this. It must be remembered that, when working with the young child, safety must be a chief concern. Pins, for example, should never be used where children could reach them. Care must be taken that toys are age-appropriate, and that toys with small parts are avoided.

An ideal preschool setting for sensory learning includes:

- child-sized tables and chairs
- large bulletin boards
- a make-believe area for role-playing and housekeeping activities
- a quiet area with picture books and manipulative story boards
- an art area
- a group gathering area with designated seating (preferably on the floor).

A prayer area set apart is a very important element of an early childhood faith-development program. This area can be provided by using a small table with a cloth over it or by simply placing a small piece of fabric on the floor in a corner of the room. A children's Bible and a candle should be included in this area.

Techniques for Making Discipline Positive

Young children need discipline in order to develop respect for themselves and others. By establishing boundaries for young children, adults help them to explore the world safely. Children who are themselves treated with respect will grow to treat others in the same way.

For discipline to be beneficial, the catechist should:

- involve the children in setting the rules for acceptable behavior in preschool
- acknowledge acceptable behavior
- target each child's strengths
- refrain from the use of negative words and gestures
- build each child's self-worth by recognizing his or her efforts
- frame expectations positively. Instead of "No noise-making in the hall," say, "Let's all walk tippy-toe, very quietly, down the hall because others are working."
- provide children a quiet place to sit in the room but away from the group. Sometimes called "time-out," this is a place for quiet re-focusing or talking things over with an adult. This place should be a place of comfort, not punishment. You as a catechist may want to sit there occasionally as you explain: "I need some time-out time! I need a quiet place to think!"

Telling a Story

Every page in the text is a page that you, as a catechist, must read to and interpret for the children. Every page is a "story" that begs to be told in an exciting and dramatic way.

This is especially true of the *Read to Me Pages*. Every effort has been made to provide a variety of songs, stories, poems, and chants for the children to listen to and participate in. Because preschoolers are not yet readers, you may want to orient them to the words on the page by moving your finger from left to right on a page that you hold up for them to see. Ask the children to follow you with their own fingers on their own pages, even if they are not on the right words.

If you have time, you may want to read the *Read to Me* selections twice. Leave words out the second time, and see whether the children can supply them. This encourages listening and comprehension. On the second reading, you may want to ask the children to listen for a particular phrase or sentence and chant it together with you or after you each time.

At the end of the story, ask questions that can be answered in more than one or two words. Ask "why?" often as this encourages thinking skills.

Then point to the pictures and ask whether the children would like to re-tell the story using the pictures. You may want to point to one section of the illustration at a time and ask, "How did the story start?" "What happened here?" "What happened next?" "Look at this picture. How did the story end?" The children will understand the story better as they review it with you and link it to the pictures. As you do so, know you are following in the footsteps of the greatest catechist and storyteller of all, Jesus Christ!

Nutrition

If your program provides time for snack, you will find ample suggestions in this guide. However, do feel free to make substitutions based on your group's needs and the preferences of families. Here are some suggestions for snacks you might like to try:

Sometimes round sugar cookies are called for in a snack. A round rice cake can be used instead.

When icing is called for in a snack, you may prefer to substitute cream cheese or another kind of cheese spread. (Cream cheese can be tinted colors, just as icing can, to contribute to a colorful snack project.)

For rectangular brown shapes (often used for tree trunks in the guide's snack suggestions), bread sticks or slices of toast cut into four rectangles can be used instead of the chocolate-covered rectangular cookies mentioned.

Raisins or carob chips are good substitutes for chocolate chips. Cereal bits in colored shapes can substitute for candies if desired.

Of course, always be aware of the children in your group who may have food allergies. Be sure to have appropriate food substitutions available for those children.

Developmental Background

Portrait of the Three-Year-Old

As you prepare to teach three-year-olds, it is important to be aware of the general characteristics that make the three-year-old unique.

- The three-year-old is very curious with a natural sense of wonder.
- The three-year-old is full of energy.
- The three-year-old possesses a short attention span.
- Three-year-olds are unable to sit still for long periods of time.
- Developing large muscles enables the three-year-old to run, hop, and jump with confidence.
- Use of crayons and scissors by the three-year-old is just beginning while stringing beads, turning knobs, and stacking blocks are more accurate.
- The three-year-old knows the difference between acceptable and unacceptable behavior.
- The three-year-old is beginning to share toys and to engage in cooperative play.
- The three-year-old asks "how" and "why" questions.
- The three-year-old can speak in simple sentences as language is developing rapidly at this age. These children are able to memorize songs, fingerplays, and enjoy rhymes.
- The three-year-old is developing a sense that boundaries and rules are an important part of daily life.
- Three-year-olds like to imitate adults and enjoy role-playing, dramatic play, and using puppets.

Portrait of the Four-Year-Old

As you prepare to teach four-year-olds, it is important to be aware of the general characteristics that make the four-year-old unique.

- The four-year-old is eager to learn about self and world.
- The four-year-old is striving for independence, but still looks to the adult for guidance.
- Large muscle activities that the four-year-old enjoys include skipping, throwing and kicking a ball, jumping rope, riding tricycles, and other physical skills that require strength and agility.
- Small muscle coordination is also developing, allowing the four-year-old more control with cutting and drawing.
- The four-year-old enjoys cooperative play and group games in which rules can be understood and followed.
- The four-year-old is able to attend to stories with greater details and to follow directions containing more steps.
- The four-year-old enjoys role-playing, as well as making up stories using puppets, stuffed animals, and props.
- Language is a tool used by four-year-olds for self-expression, for interaction with others, and for getting what they want.
- Four-year-olds are concerned with cause-and-effect relationships.
- Four-year-olds enjoy the repetition in songs and fingerplays.

Developmental Background

Portrait of the Five-Year-Old

As you prepare to teach five-year-olds, it is important to be aware of the general characteristics that make the five-year-old unique.

- The five-year-old is eager to be involved in the learning process.
- These children possess a heightened level of independence and desire to make decisions on their own.
- Because five-year-olds are experiencing many changes in their world, rules provide a source of stability. Intolerance for breaking the rules is common.
- The five-year-old enjoys greater physical coordination and is able to participate in activities requiring more skill.
- Using a pencil, coloring within the lines, and cutting become more accurate, although continued practice is still necessary.
- The five-year-old is social and enjoys cooperative play and formal group games. Winning, losing, and working together become meaningful concepts.
- Though their interests are moving toward understanding the real world, five-year-olds still enjoy dramatic play, fantasy, and puppets.
- Language becomes a tool for the five-year-old to express feelings, thoughts, fears, and wants.
- The five-year-old enjoys music and is able to add movement and motions to this experience.

Tools and Tips

Working With Preschool Children

Teaching the preschool child provides the opportunity for the catechist to participate in a young child's sense of wonder and enthusiasm. The following tools and tips are helpful:

- Involve the child in the learning process.
- Provide a variety of materials, toys, games, and equipment that encourage cooperative play and creativity. Include simple puzzles, large blocks, paints, play-dough, clay, puppets, and stuffed animals.
- Provide opportunities for both formal and spontaneous prayer.
- Alternate movement and quiet activities.
- Provide a variety of experiences involving as many senses as possible.
- Establish eye contact when speaking to or listening to children.
- Focus on the *process* of the learning activities rather than the final product.
- Be prepared; review the lesson to be taught ahead of time.
- Use storytelling throughout the lesson and allow for dramatization by the children.
- Use music, fingerplays, songs, and action rhymes to involve the child in the learning process.
- Be flexible and spontaneous, sharing your sense of humor.

An extra tip from Sadlier: Classroom libraries are available in Little Books/Big Books format to further support the themes of the lessons. Two collections appropriate as Read-to-Me selections for preschool are Lee Bennett Hopkins' *Mother Goose* and *Worlds of Poetry*. Call 1-800-221-5175.

Ready? Set? Go!
(How the Lessons Work)

The Child's Text

To acquaint yourself with the program, briefly flip through the child's text. You will notice that the pages are meant to be removed and used separately. The Guide offers clear directions for using each page of the text.

Units

Looking at the Table of Contents in the child's text, you will note that the entire book is divided into four units. Each unit revolves around a season of the year, and integrates the important liturgical seasons and holy days celebrated by the Church. Holidays significant to family life, such as Halloween, Thanksgiving, Mother's Day, and Father's Day, are also taught in the text.

Lessons

The first five lessons of each unit are core lessons, based on a central faith-development theme. The remaining three lessons can be integrated as needed into your calendar.

Each lesson consists of three parts. Part 1 introduces the concept to be taught; Part 2 develops the concept through active learning; Part 3 summarizes, reviews, and reinforces the concept through the *Read to Me Page* for the children and the *Parenting Page* (on its reverse side) for the parents.

The Guide

The Guide devotes two pages to each part of a lesson. The parts are clearly marked at the top of the guide pages. The first page presents the basics: Theme, Purpose, Beginning, Middle, and End. On the flip side, the *Extra! Extra! Page* offers additional ideas and suggestions to enhance the lesson further.

The Theme and Purpose provide the focus for the lesson you will be presenting. The Beginning leads the children into the lesson theme. The Middle presents the *Activity Page* or *Read to Me Page* to be used for that lesson. The End helps the young child experience and internalize the concepts taught and concludes the lesson with a prayer experience.

The Parenting Page

Each lesson concludes with a *Parenting Page*. This is *not* for parents only! You, as a catechist, are urged to read the *Parenting Page* as well, as it provides important background to the theme of the lesson and to the developmental issues of the child. Be sure to send the *Parenting Page* home at the end of the lesson.

Ready? Set? Go!

Options for Using the Discovering God Program

Catechetical Setting	Time	Program Outline
Parish Religious Education Programs Early Childhood Programs	One day per week	Use Parts 1 and 2 of each lesson including the corresponding *Activity Pages*; include at least one art, music, or movement activity from the lesson. Send home the *Read to Me Page* for Part 3 with the *Parenting Page* on the back.
Catholic School Preschool Programs Daycare Centers	Two days per week	On the first day use Part 1. On the second day use Part 2. Include at least one art, music, or movement activity from the lesson each day. Include *Extra! Extra!* activities as time allows. Send home the *Read to Me Page* for Part 3 with the *Parenting Page* on the back.
Catholic School Preschool Programs Daycare Centers	Three days per week	On the first day use Part 1. On the second day use Part 2. On the third day use Part 3. Include at least one art, music, or movement activity from the lesson each day. Include *Extra! Extra!* activities as time allows. Send home the *Read to Me Page* for Part 3 with the *Parenting Page* on the back.
Catholic School Preschool Programs Daycare Centers	Five days per week	On the first day use Part 1. On the second day, review and reinforce Part 1 with *Extra! Extra!* activities from Part 1. On the third day use Part 2. On the fourth day, review and reinforce Part 2 with *Extra! Extra!* activities from Part 2. On the fifth day, use Part 3. Include *Extra! Extra!* activities as time allows. Send home the *Read to Me Page* and the *Parenting Page*.

Unit 1
God Gives Us Friends

Theme: Celebrating Fall

Beginning

A small tree should be attached to the wall at the children's eye level. Prepare a fall leaf from red, yellow, or orange construction paper for each child with his or her name on it. As each child enters the preschool room, he or she should find the leaf with his or her name on it and attach it to the tree. (This tree remains up all year. The symbols with names on them change with the changes of the seasons.) This tree will help symbolize that, while each child is an individual, he or she is also part of a larger Church community.

Introduce the season of fall by bringing in items that are particular to this time of year. Some items might include a sweater, a rake, apples, leaves, pumpkins, a soccer ball, a football, and so on. Gather the children and show them these objects. Talk about the season of fall. Explain that as the weather starts to get cooler, the leaves begin to turn color and fall off the trees.

Teach the children the following song:

♪ **Fall is Here** *(To the tune of "Frère Jacques")*

Fall is here, fall is here.
Grab your rake! Grab your rake!
Colored leaves and pumpkins, colored leaves and pumpkins!
Celebrate! Celebrate!

Middle

Pass out a copy of the *Unit Page* to each child. Explain that the pictures show people having fun doing things in the fall. Invite the children to make up a story about each picture. Ask the children what they like to do in the fall.

End

 Make a fall tree. Give each child an empty paper towel spool. Have the children paint this brown. Cut several slits in the top and bend the strips outward to form branches. Have the children put a thin layer of glue on these branches. Give the children yellow, orange, and red tissue paper squares. Show them how to crumple the tissue squares and stick them onto the glue-covered branches.

Prepare "Fabulous Fall Trees" together. Give each child a rice cake. Have the children use popsicle sticks or plastic knives to cover this with softened cream cheese. To make the colorful leaves, give the children grated or shredded carrots, celery slices, and pieces of pimentos to add on the cream cheese. Give each child a fat pretzel stick to use as a tree trunk. Enjoy with apple juice.

Note: Be aware of any children with food allergies before using this activity.

Extra! Extra!

 A Handprint Fall Tree
Paint each child's forearm brown (the tree-trunk) and stamp this onto a piece of white construction paper. Paint the child's hand (with fingers open wide) yellow, orange, and red. Help the child stamp this at the top of the trunk to complete the tree.

 Read any of the following books:

When Autumn Comes, by Robert Maass, published by Henry Holt & Company, Inc., (New York) 1992.

Autumn Days, by Ann Schweninger, published by Puffin Books (New York) 1993.

Autumn, by Gerda Muller, published by Gryphon House, (Beltsville, MD) 1994.

Additional Suggestions for Storytime During Unit 1

Bridwell, Norman. *Clifford's Thanksgiving Visit.* New York: Scholastic, Inc., 1993.

Brown, Marc. *Arthur's Thanksgiving.* New York: Little Brown & Company, 1984.

Dalgliesh, Alice. *The Thanksgiving Story.* New York: Simon & Schuster Children's Books, 1988.

dePaola, Tomie. *Francis, the Poor Man of Assisi.* New York: Holiday House Publishing, 1990.

Freeman, Don. *Corduroy.* New York: Puffin Books, 1972.

Kroll, Steven. *Oh, What a Thanksgiving!* New York: Scholastic, Inc., 1988.

McGovern, Ann. *The Pilgrims' First Thanksgiving.* New York: Scholastic, Inc., 1993.

Rogers, Jacqueline. *Best Friends Sleep Over.* New York: Scholastic, Inc. 1993.

Sasso, Sandy Eisenberg. *God's Paintbrush.* Woodstock, VT: Jewish Lights Publishing, 1992.

Waters, Kate. *Samuel Eaton's Day: A Day in the Life of a Pilgrim Boy.* New York: Scholastic, Inc., 1996.

_____. *Sarah Morton's Day: A Day in the Life of a Pilgrim Girl.* New York: Scholastic, Inc., 1993.

 **Materials for Lesson 1, Part 1:**
- *Activity Page 3*
- Sudie Squirrel
- construction paper
- yarn
- basket
- instant camera

Theme: Welcome to our kindergarten.

Purpose:
• *to help the children experience belonging to a special community, their kindergarten group.*

Beginning

Have a tree attached to the wall or bulletin board at the children's eye level as suggested in the lesson for the *Unit Page.* Attach Sudie Squirrel to the tree. Prepare a red, yellow, or orange leaf for each child with his or her name on it. As each child enters the room, welcome him or her. After the children come in, help them find the leaves with their names on them and attach them to the tree. Make some construction paper acorns and string a piece of yarn through a hole in the top of each one. Put each child's name on one acorn and save these for an activity in the **End** section of this lesson. Appropriate toys such as puzzles, large snap-together blocks, books, clay, and so on, should be out on the tables for the children to play with as they arrive.

Gather the children in a circle or group. Take Sudie Squirrel from the tree and introduce her to the group. As you do this, have each child tell Sudie Squirrel his or her name.

Explain that this year we will do many exciting things together. We are going to learn about God and his love for us. We will learn about God's only Son, Jesus, who is our friend. We will play games, sing songs, and listen to stories. Emphasize that we will all become friends.

Middle
Show *Activity Page 3* to the children. Read aloud the message at the top of the page. Tell the children that they are going to make a sign that shows they are in kindergarten. Help the children print their names on the yellow sign. Take a picture of each child using an instant camera. Show the children how to cut out their pictures and paste them on their signs.

End
Gather the children in a circle or group. Teach the following song:

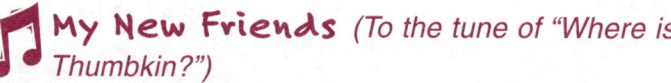
My New Friends *(To the tune of "Where is Thumbkin?")*

There is (friend's name).	**We belong together**
There is (friend's name).	**In our kindergarten.**
He's (She's) my friend.	**Let's be friends.**
He's (She's) my friend.	**Let's be friends.**

Provide Sudie Squirrel with a basket of the acorn name tags. Have Sudie Squirrel explain that acorns are her favorite food and that she would like to share these with her new friends. As each child's name is sung in the song, have Sudie Squirrel put the child's nametag around his or her neck.

Gather the children around the prayer table. Explain that this is a special place in our room where we gather each day to talk to God and offer a prayer. Lead the children in the following prayer: "Dear God, thank you for all our new friends. Amen."

Extra! Extra!

 **Welcome Friends**

Make a hat or a hair bow from construction paper for each child. Put the children's names on these. Provide each child with a small paper plate on which a face has already been drawn. Let the children glue on the appropriate color of crinkle paper to make hair. Then have the children find the hat or hair bow with their names on them and attach these to the paper plate "people." Tell the children that they will hang their pictures near the tree so that Sudie Squirrel can look at them when the children are at home. Help the children attach these paper plate "people" to the wall under the tree.

Materials for Part 2:
- *Activity Page 4*
- yarn or ribbon
- empty film containers
- paint

Hooray for New Friends (Part 2)

Theme: The sign of the cross is a special sign of God's love.

Purpose:
• *to introduce the children to the sign of the cross as a special sign of God's love.*

Beginning
As the children enter the room, have Sudie Squirrel welcome them. Then help the children find the leaves with their names on them and place them on the tree.

Gather the children in a circle or group. Sing the song "My New Friends" found on page 16 with the children. Have Sudie Squirrel put the nametags on the children again as their names are sung. Then explain that we have another friend—Jesus. Sing the song, inserting Jesus' name for the friend's name.

Middle
Pass out a copy of *Activity Page 4* to each child. Read the words at the top of the page aloud. Help the children cut out the squares at the bottom of the page. Help the children arrange them in the proper sequence by matching the numbers on the pictures with the numbers on the sign. Once the pictures are in the correct places, have the children glue them down. Then have the children cut out their signs. Punch a hole in the sign and thread a piece of yarn or ribbon through the hole. Tie the ends of the yarn or ribbon and let the children wear their signs home. Remind the children that the first side of their sign shows they belong in kindergarten and the second side of the sign shows they are loved by God.

End
Help the children make a cross for the prayer table. Cut a large cross from a piece of poster board. Let each child make a face on the cross by dipping an empty film container in paint and printing a circle on the cross. Help the children add facial features and hair. Let this dry, then place it on the prayer table.

Practice making the sign of the cross with the children (being sure to mirror this for them). Conclude by leading the children in the prayer found on the bottom of *Activity Page 4.*

18

Extra! Extra!

 A Cross Necklace

Help each child make a cross necklace to wear. For each child, cut a small cross from colorful craft foam and punch a hole in the top. String a piece of yarn or ribbon through the hole and tie to make a necklace. Have each child glue one sequin on each of the four ends of the cross. When this has dried, practice making the sign of the cross by having the children touch the appropriate sequin as the prayer is said. Let the children wear these necklaces home.

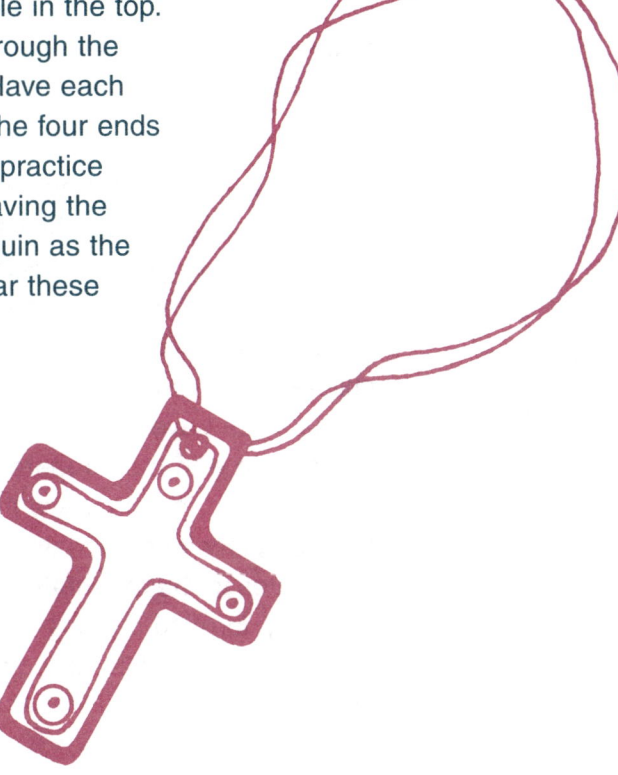

Materials for Part 3:
- *Read to Me* Page 5
- graham crackers
- icing
- candy-coated chocolates

Hooray for New Friends (Part 3)

Theme: We are happy to have new friends and to be loved by God.

Purpose:
• *to help the children identify and talk about their feelings as they experience belonging to their new kindergarten group.*

Beginning

As the children enter the room, have Sudie Squirrel welcome them. Then help the children find the leaves with their names on them and place them on the tree.

Gather the children in a circle on the floor. Act out the following situations using Sudie Squirrel and ask the children the questions after each one.

- Sudie is trying to work a puzzle, but cannot finish it because she cannot find one of the pieces. (It is behind her and she cannot see it). What would friends do?

- Sudie has a ball and a mitt but cannot play baseball by herself. What would friends do?

- Sudie has brought a special snack for the children (a box of graham crackers) but it is too heavy for her to carry. What would friends do?

After the situations have been discussed, act them out again, this time letting a child come and help Sudie.

Middle

Pass out a copy of *Read to Me Page 5* to each child. Draw the children's attention to the illustrations. Introduce the story by reminding the children that they are just beginning to belong to their kindergarten group and are making many friends. Tell the children that this is a story about Joey and his first day in kindergarten. Read the story aloud, encouraging the children to look at the illustrations as you read. Then ask the question at the bottom of the page. Invite all the children to participate in the discussion.

End

Let the children enjoy a special snack. Give each child a graham cracker from the box that Sudie brought. Have them spread icing on the graham crackers. Then lead the children in praying the Sign of the Cross. Then have them trace a cross in the icing with their fingers. After they lick their fingers, have the children place candy-coated chocolates in the indentation left in the icing, forming a cross with the candies. Let the children enjoy their snack. *Note: Be aware of any children with food allergies before using this activity.*

Gather the children around the prayer table. Lead them in the following prayer: "Dear God, thank you for all our new friends in kindergarten. Amen."

Extra! Extra!

 The End-of-Year Scrapbook

Make a scrapbook for each child that can be added to throughout the year. Take a picture of each child with Sudie Squirrel. Mount this on a piece of construction paper. Write the date and the words *Sudie Squirrel is my brand new friend in my kindergarten.*

Save these pages in a separate folder for each child to bind together at the end of the year.

September 10
Sudie Squirrel is my brand new friend in my kindergarten.

 **Materials for Lesson 2, Part 1:**
- *Activity Page 7*
- ball

Theme: Our names say to whom we belong.

Purpose:
• *to affirm that each child is special by stressing the importance of the child's name, and to further deepen the child's experience of belonging.*

Beginning

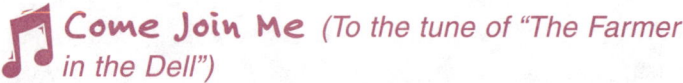 As the children enter the room, have Sudie Squirrel welcome them. Then help the children find the leaves with their names on them and place them on the tree.

Make the outline of a tree using masking tape on the floor. Gather the children around the tree on the floor. Have Sudie Squirrel and yourself sitting in the tree. Sing the following song, inserting each child's name.

🎵 **Come Join Me** *(To the tune of "The Farmer in the Dell")*

Come join me in my tree.
Come join me in my tree.
I'll be happy as can be
If (child's name) will join me.

After all the children have had a turn to come sit in the tree, ask them how they knew it was their turn. (*Because of their names!*)

Middle
Pass out a copy of *Activity Page 7* to each child. Read aloud the words at the top of the page. Help the children print their first and last names in the spaces provided. Explain that their last names tell what families they belong to. Then read the lines at the bottom of the page.

End
Gather the children in a circle on the floor. Play the game, "Roll, Ball, Roll" with them. Take a ball and say, "My name is _____, and I am going to roll the ball to _____." Roll the ball to that child. Instruct all the children to wave to that child and say, "Hello, _____." Then have that child roll the ball back to you. Continue around the circle until all the children have had a turn. (Note: Sudie Squirrel should also have a turn.)

Gather the children around the prayer table and lead them in the following prayer: "Dear God, thank you for making me special, and for giving me a family to belong to. Amen."

22

Extra! Extra!

 A Book of Friends

Give each child a piece of tagboard 4" by 11". Write each child's name with glue on his or her tagboard. Have the children sprinkle colored salt on the glue and let dry. (You can have one made for Sudie ahead of time.) Give each child six pieces of newsprint 4" by 11". Have them use one of these pieces to make a crayon rubbing of their own names. Then have them go around the room and make a crayon rubbing of five other children's names. Staple these together with the child's own name on top.

Materials for Part 2:
- *Activity Page 8*
- water in a pitcher

23

What is Your Name? (Part 2)

Theme: We belong to a special family.

Purpose:
• *to deepen the children's sense of belonging by introducing a special family, the Catholic Church.*

Beginning
As the children enter the room, have Sudie Squirrel welcome them. Then help the children find the leaves with their names on them and place them on the tree.

Gather the children in a circle on the floor. Explain that when they were very small, they were baptized, making them members of the Catholic Church family. Remind the children that they have been baptized and are now children of God. Call up each child by name, one at a time. Using a pitcher, pour a small amount of water on his or her hand and say, "(child's name), you are a child of God." Continue in this way until each child has had a turn.

Middle
Pass out a copy of *Activity Page 8* to each child. Read the message at the top of the page to the children.

Ask the children to look at the sign. Read the quote from Isaiah to the children. Tell the children that God knows each one of them.

Then call the children's attention to the pictures on the sign. Explain that the pictures on the sign are symbols of Baptism. Have the children cut out the sign and fold it on the line indicated (page 7).

End
Have the children bring their name cards to the prayer table. Remind the children that when they were babies they were baptized into the Catholic Church family. We use the cross as a sign that we belong to this special family. Help the children arrange their name cards in the shape of a cross on the prayer table. (If the table is too small, the cards can be placed in the shape of a cross on the floor near the prayer table.)

Gather the children around the prayer table. Lead them in the prayer found at the bottom of *Activity Page 8.*

Extra! Extra!

Glue A Sign of Love and Belonging

Help the children make wooden crosses. Give each child two popsicle sticks. Help them glue the two sticks together to form a cross. Help the children write their names on the crosses. Remind the children that the cross is a sign of God's love. It is a sign that we belong to a special family, the Church. Let the children bring their crosses home.

Camille

Materials for Part 3:
- *Read to Me Page 9*
- birthday candles
- stamp pad
- construction paper

What is Your Name?
(Part 3)

Theme: We belong to a special family.

Purpose:
• *to help the children understand that at Baptism they were welcomed into a special family, the Catholic Church.*

Beginning
As the children enter the room, have Sudie Squirrel welcome them. Then help the children find the leaves with their names on them and place them on the tree.

Gather the children in a circle on the floor. Remind the children that we have been talking about Baptism, when they became members of a special family, the Catholic Church. On that day, their families received a special candle as a reminder that the light of Jesus is shining in their hearts from that day on. Lead the children in the following prayer service. You may also want to give each child a small unlit birthday candle to hold during the song as a reminder of the light of Christ.

Leader: We are children of God.

All: ♫ **Shine Your Light** (*To the tune of "Row, Row, Row Your Boat"*)
Shine, shine, shine your light
For everyone to see.
Thank you, Jesus, for your light
Shining now in me.

Leader: We belong to a special family. (*All: Song verse*)
Leader: We belong to the Catholic Church. (*All: Song verse*)
Leader: Jesus gave us his light. (*All: Song verse*)

Middle
Pass out a copy of *Read to Me Page 9* to each child. Have the children look at the pictures and tell what the people are doing. Encourage the children to listen carefully as you read the story.

When finished, ask the children whether they know about their own Baptism day. Perhaps they have seen some pictures. Ask whether any of them have been to the Baptism of a younger brother or sister. Let the children share their experiences of Baptism.

End
Add a page to each child's scrapbook. On a piece of construction paper, draw a cross or a candle. Have the children dip their thumbs in stamp pads and make thumbprints around the cross or candle for people that  were probably at their Baptism. Help the children draw faces on these people and label them with names. Write on the bottom of the page the words *(child's name), I have called you by name.*

 Gather the children around the prayer table. Teach them the following fingerplay, adding the motions as they say it.

Praying
Open, shut them. Open, shut them. (*Open and close hands.*)
Fold your hands in prayer. (*Fold hands in the praying position.*)
God will hear, (*Raise arms up high.*)
And God will care. (*Open arms wide.*)
God is with us everywhere. (*Open arms wide.*)
(*Repeat lines 1 and 2.*)

Extra! Extra!

A Baptismal Party

Tell the children that when they were baptized their families held a celebration to welcome them into the special family of the Catholic Church. Provide a plain sheet cake with white icing. Write all the children's names on the cake using gel icing. Explain that all the children's names are on the cake because they are members of this special family. Cut and serve the cake and provide juice to drink.

Note: Be aware of any children with food allergies before using this activity.

Materials for Lesson 3, Part 1:
- *Activity Page 11*
- shoe box treasure chest
- a tub of sand or salt
- yarn or string
- variously colored pony beads

Theme: We are learning how to be good friends.

Purpose:
• *to help the children acquire the social skills necessary for being and having friends.*

Beginning
Ahead of time, make a treasure chest using a shoe box. Prepare medallions for each child: Cut small circles from gold or yellow poster board and write each child's name on one. Punch a hole in the top. "Bury" these in a tub of sand or salt.

As the children enter the room, have Sudie Squirrel welcome them. Then help the children find the leaves with their names on them and place them on the tree.

Gather the children in a circle on the floor. Tell the children that God has given us great treasure. Ask them whether they can guess what the treasure is. Show the children the empty treasure chest. Tell the children that we will have to dig for treasure to fill the chest. Let each child have a turn digging for and finding one medallion and putting the medallion in the treasure chest. When all the medallions have been found, tell the children that now we have great treasure—each one of us. Explain that friends are great treasures.

Middle
Pass out a copy of *Activity Page 11* to each child. Have the children look at the two pictures. Discuss each picture, asking for volunteers to make up a story about what is happening in the picture. Invite the children to use the blank circle to draw and color their own story about what friends do. After the children have finished, ask for volunteers to share their stories with the group. Encourage all the children to take a turn sharing.

End
Provide yarn or string and various colors of "pony" beads (available in craft stores). Help the children make necklaces using the beads. Have the children add the medallions with their names on them to their necklaces. Tie the ends of the yarn or string together when the children have completed their necklaces.

Have the children place their necklaces in the treasure chest and bring the chest to the prayer table. Gather the children around the prayer table and lead them in the following prayer: "Dear God, thank you for making our group a treasure of friends. Amen."

Extra! Extra!

Read the story *Best Friends Sleep Over* by Jacqueline Rogers. Talk about all the fun things the friends did together. Ask the children how Ricky showed he was a friend to Gilbert. How did Gilbert show he was a friend to Ricky?

Materials for Part 2:
- *Activity Page 12*
- tagboard "jewels"
- glitter
- yarn

Being Friends (Part 2)

Theme: Good friends bring God's love.

Purpose:
• *to help the children appreciate that God's love comes to us through our friends.*

Beginning

 As the children enter the room, have Sudie Squirrel welcome them. Then help the children find the leaves with their names on them and place them on the tree.

Gather the children in a circle on the floor. Show the children the treasure chest. Remind them that we have a treasure of friends in our group. Tell the children that treasures need to be shared. Explain that we will make something to share with a friend. Give each child a jewel shape cut from tagboard with a hole punched at the top. Help the children decorate these with glitter.

Middle

Pass out a copy of *Activity Page 12* to each child. Read the first two lines to the children. Stress that friends bring us God's love in many different ways, and we bring God's love to our friends in our own special ways.

Ask the children to make the faces on the page look like three different friends. Then help the children cut out the faces. Punch a hole at the top of each face and string a piece of yarn through it. Let the children hang these on the tree where they hang their leaves with their names, or provide a separate Friendship Tree.

End

Gather the children around the prayer table with the jewels made in the beginning of this lesson. Encourage the children to share their jewels with another child in the group. As each child gives his or her jewel to another child, slip a safety pin through the hole and pin this jewel to the child. Be sure all the children end up with one shared jewel. Explain to the children that our beautiful treasure is not in the treasure chest but all around us. Then lead the children in the prayer found on the bottom of *Activity Page 12.*

Extra! Extra!

Tasty Treasures

Give each child a small amount of treasure (chocolate chips, candy-coated chocolates, butterscotch chips, and so on). Tell the children that they should share their treasure, and provide a bowl for them to put their treasure in. Then tell them we will bury our treasure. Provide each child with a graham cracker in a small zippered bag. Have the children crush the graham cracker in the bag then pour this on top of the treasure in the bowl. Scoop some of the buried treasure into cups for the children to enjoy.

Note: Be aware of any children with food allergies before using this activity.

Review the story *Best Friends Sleep Over*. Then provide pieces of scrap fabric about 12" by 12" for each child. Explain that we will make blankets for a sleep over. Let the children decorate the fabric using fabric markers, sponges and fabric paint, or permanent markers. Keep the blankets for an additional activity in Part 3.

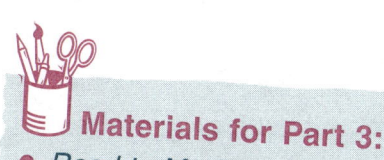

Materials for Part 3:
- *Read to Me Page 13*
- poster board
- tempera paint

Being Friends (Part 3)

Theme: Good friends love God and love one another, too.

Purpose:
• *to nurture the child's positive attitudes towards, and ability to cooperate with, friends.*

Beginning
As the children enter the room, have Sudie Squirrel welcome them. Then help the children find the leaves with their names on them and place them on the tree.

Gather the children in a circle on the floor. Teach them the following fingerplay, including the motions.

Ten Helpful Fingers
I have ten little fingers (*Hold up ten fingers.*)
That God gave to me.
Together they can do things (*Clasp hands together.*)
They can't do separately. (*Separate clasped hands and wiggle fingers.*)

I can fold them when I pray, (*Fold hands in prayer.*)
Or share with friends at play, (*Extend hands to friend.*)
Carry big bags from the store, (*Pretend to hold a big bag.*)
Be a helper at the door. (*Pretend to open the door.*)
When ten fingers work together, (*Hold up ten fingers.*)
They make us feel much better. (*Hug self.*)

Middle
Pass out a copy of *Read to Me Page 13* to the children. Draw the children's attention to the pictures that show children being good friends to one another. Ask for volunteers to tell you what is happening in each of the pictures. Ask the children to listen and to look at the illustrations as you read the poem.

After you have read the poem, ask the children whether they have ever done any of the things mentioned with or for a friend. Stress that good friends love God and love one another, too.

End
On a large poster board, draw the outline of a treasure chest. Help the children paint their hands with tempera paint and print their handprints in the treasure chest. Explain that each of us is a treasure, and we can use our hands to share the treasure of ourselves.

Gather the children around the prayer table. Place the poster of the treasure chest with handprints on the prayer table. Lead the children in the following prayer: "Dear God, help us to bring God's love to everyone we meet. Amen."

Extra! Extra!

Real Treasures

Make a treasure chest magnet for the refrigerator. For each child, draw the outline of a treasure chest on tagboard and cut out. Help the children dip their thumbs into a stamp pad and put one thumbprint inside the treasure chest for each child in the group. Attach a piece of magnetic strip to the back. Encourage the children to bring these home and put them on their refrigerators to remind them that friends are real treasures, and that we have to continue to share ourselves.

A Sleep Over

Review the story *Best Friends Sleep Over.* Tell the children that we will have a pretend sleep over. Have the children bring their stuffed animals from home or use some that are available in the room. Have the children cover the stuffed animals with the blankets made previously. Do some of the activities from the story. Read the children a bedtime story. Let the children pretend to go to sleep.

Materials for Lesson 4, Part 1:
- *Activity Page 15*
- a bag with objects such as: an adhesive bandage, a small broom, a vase of flowers, a book, a puzzle, a box of crayons

Theme: Many people love and care for us.

Purpose:
• to help the children experience helping others, giving and receiving love.

Beginning

As the children enter the room, have Sudie Squirrel welcome them. Then help the children find the leaves with their names on them and place them on the tree.

Gather the children in a circle on the floor. Remind them that God created all of us. Explain that God loves each one of us the same, so we should love everyone the same. Tell the children that God wants us to show our love for one another. We can do this by loving and helping one another.

Play a "Help One Another" game. Fill a bag with objects or pictures of objects that could be used to help others. Some examples include an adhesive bandage, a small broom, a vase of flowers, a book, a puzzle, and a box of crayons. Invite one child to come up and reach into the bag and pull out an object or picture. Encourage the child to tell how he or she could use it to help someone. Possible responses might be: "I could take the vase of flowers to someone who is sick or sad"; "I could give the bandage to a friend with a skinned knee"; "I could use the broom to help my mom keep the house clean." Be sure to give each child the opportunity to have a turn.

Middle

Pass out a copy of *Activity Page 15* to the children. Draw the children's attention to the puppets. Invite the children to use their crayons to make one of their puppets look like themselves. Encourage them to make the other puppet look like one of their friends. Read the message at the bottom of the page to the children.

End

Gather the children in a circle or group. Teach them the following song:

🎵 **Helping Hands** *(To the tune of "Here We Go 'Round the Mulberry Bush")*

Here are my two little helping hands,
My two helping hands, my two helping hands.
Here are my two little helping hands,
To show how much I love God.

I use my two hands in so many ways,
In so many ways, in so many ways.
I use my two hands in so many ways
To show how much I love you.

Gather the children around the prayer table and lead them in the following prayer: "Dear God, thank you for all the people who love us. Help us to show love for one another by loving and helping each other. Amen." Conclude by singing the "Helping Hands" song.

Extra! Extra!

 Read the book *Corduroy* by Don Freeman. Ask the children how Lisa showed love to Corduroy. Did Corduroy show love to Lisa, too? (*He became her friend and she wasn't lonely anymore.*)

Materials for Part 2:
- *Activity Page 16*
- construction paper
- sticky velcro
- carpet square

Helping Friends
(Part 2)

Theme: God wants us to be good friends to others and to bring them God's love.

Purpose:
• *to help the children understand that we show we love others by what we say and do.*

Beginning

As the children enter the room, have Sudie Squirrel welcome them. Then help the children find the leaves with their names on them and place them on the tree.

Trace each child's hand on a piece of construction paper and cut out. Attach a piece of sticky velcro to the back of this hand. Have the children gather in a circle on the floor with their construction paper hands. Explain to the children that we can show love to other people when we help them. Then go around the circle of children inviting each child to tell something he or she could do to help someone else or to show God's love to someone. As the children suggest something they could do, have them bring their construction paper hands up and stick them on a carpet square in the front of the group. When everyone has had a turn, and the carpet square is full of hands, comment "We have a group of helping hands!"

Middle

Pass out a copy of *Activity Page 16* to the children. Read the message at the top of the page to the children. Invite the children to finish the puppets and then cut them out. Help the children as needed. Have the children cut out the bands at the bottom of the page. Staple each band into a circle and attach to a puppet. Show the children how to put their fingers in the bands to make finger puppets. Encourage the children to use their puppets to act out situations of showing God's love to each other.

End

Give each child his or her construction paper hand used in the beginning of this lesson. Help the children glue glitter on the hands and let dry. Then put the hands in the treasure chest and bring to the prayer table. Explain to the children that friends who show God's love to each other are truly valuable treasures.

Gather the children around the prayer table and lead them in the prayer found on the bottom of *Activity Page 16.*

Extra! Extra!

 **A Love Button**

Review the story *Corduroy.* Remind the children that Lisa showed love to Corduroy by saving her money to buy him and then by sewing a button on his overalls. Invite the children to show love by using a button to make a picture for their parents. Give each child a button and have him or her glue this on a piece of construction paper. Then have the children use markers to turn this into a beautiful picture.

Materials for Part 3:
- *Read to Me Page 17*
- tempera paint
- paper squares
- basket of fruit
- large bowl

Helping Friends
(Part 3)

Theme: We are learning how to be good friends to others.

Purpose:

• *to encourage the children to find ways to show love to others.*

Beginning

As the children enter the room, have Sudie Squirrel welcome them. Then help the children find the leaves with their names on them and place them on the tree.

Gather the children in a circle or group. Remind them that we can use our hands to help others and in this way we are showing God's love to them. Then paint both hands of each child with tempera paint and "print" them on a square piece of paper. Make a "Helping Hands" quilt by joining all the squares together to form a "quilt." Hang this in the kindergarten room to remind the children to find ways to show love to others.

Middle

Pass out a copy of *Read to Me Page 17* to the children. Draw the children's attention to the illustrations surrounding the story. Have the children listen carefully as you read each situation. After reading each situation, ask the question, "What would a true friend do?" Invite all the children to participate in the discussion.

End

Provide a basket of real fruit. Have each child pick one fruit from the basket to share with the whole group. Cut up this fruit and place in a large bowl. Continue with all the fruits chosen by the children. Give each child a cupful of "Friendship Fruit Salad" to enjoy. Share some of this fruit salad with another teacher or person in the school. *Note: Be aware of any children with food allergies before using this activity.*

Gather the children around the prayer table. Lead them in the following prayer: "Dear God, thank you for giving us friends to share with. Amen."

Extra! Extra!

Teddy Bear Toast

Review the story *Corduroy* with the children. Then have the children bring their teddy bears to school (or provide some from the room). Go outside and have a picnic. Serve "Teddy Bear Toast." Cut slices of toast with a bear-shaped cookie cutter. Sprinkle on cinnamon and sugar.

Note: Be aware of any children with food allergies before using this activity.

Materials for Lesson 5, Part 1:
- *Activity Page 19*
- props such as books, toys, food, blankets, bandages, sponges, and soap
- red poster board
- pictures of community helpers
- tagboard
- marbles and paint
- community helpers stickers

Theme: We can trust good friends who love and care for us.

Purpose:
• *to introduce the children to the concepts of caring and trusting.*

Beginning

As the children enter the room, have Sudie Squirrel welcome them. Then help the children find the leaves with their names on them and place them on the tree.

Gather the children in a circle on the floor. Show them Sudie Squirrel. Tell the children that we need to take care of Sudie. Ask the children to think of some things that need to be done to take care of her. Have some props such as books, toys, food, blankets, bandages, sponge and soap, and so on available for use by the children. Let the children suggest things such as feeding, bathing, hugging, and playing together. As the children suggest these things, encourage them to use the available props to pretend to take care of Sudie.

Middle

Pass out a copy of *Activity Page 19* to each child. Read the paragraph at the top of the page to the children. Invite the children to tell who takes care of them and whom they trust. Then have the children look at the four pictures, one at a time. Invite volunteers to tell what is happening in each picture. Ask the children whether the adult in the picture can be trusted. Include all the children in the discussion.

End

Prepare a large red heart from poster board. Glue pictures of community helpers on the heart. Cut this heart into puzzle pieces with each piece having a picture on it. Have the children work together to put the puzzle together. Explain that God has given us all these people to take care of us and to show us his love.

Invite the children to make individual heart puzzles to take home. Give each child a piece of tagboard with a heart drawn on it. Have them place this inside a box lid. Dip marbles in various colors of tempera paint. Place these marbles in the box lid on top of the tagboard. Have the children tip the box lid causing the marbles to roll around leaving trails of paint. Remove the marbles and allow to dry. When the heart is dry, cut it out and cut into five pieces. Give the children community helpers stickers and have them place one sticker on each piece. Put the pieces in an envelope or zippered plastic bag to take home.

Gather the children around the prayer table. Bring the big red heart puzzle. Lead the children in the following prayer: "Dear God, thank you for giving us good friends who love and care for us. Amen."

Extra! Extra!

♫ People Who Care for Me
(To the tune of "Mary Had a Little Lamb")

God gives people who care for me,
Care for me,
Care for me.
God gives people who care for me.
They're a special gift, you see.

My parents love and comfort me,
Comfort me,
Comfort me.
My parents love and comfort me.
They're a special gift, you see.

My teacher always reads to me,
Reads to me,
Reads to me.
My teacher always reads to me.
She's (he's) a special gift, you see.

The parish priest says Mass for me,
Mass for me,
Mass for me.
The parish priest says Mass for me.
He's a special gift, you see.

The farmer grows the food for me,
Food for me,
Food for me.
The farmer grows the food for me.
He's (She's) a special gift, you see.

The doctor helps me when I'm sick,
When I'm sick,
When I'm sick.
The doctor helps me when I'm sick.
He's (she's) a special gift, you see.

The police officer keeps me safe from harm,
Safe from harm,
Safe from harm.
The police officer keeps me safe from harm;
He's (She's) a special gift, you see.

Materials for Part 2:
- *Activity Page 19*
- *Activity Page 20*
- construction paper

Trusting Friends (Part 2)

Theme: We can trust people who know and love us.

Purpose:
• *to build the concepts of caring and trusting.*

Beginning

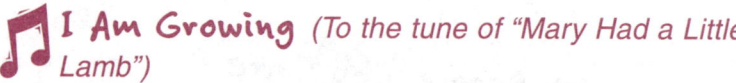 As the children enter the room, have Sudie Squirrel welcome them. Then help the children find the leaves with their names on them and place them on the tree.

Set up a small town in the kindergarten room. Have several areas set up around the room where the children can play and pretend to be helpers in the community. Some suggestions include a barber shop/beauty salon, a restaurant, a library, a hospital, and a bus. Allow the children time to explore these centers and pretend they are the community helpers. As the children play in the various areas, take their pictures using an instant camera. Save these pictures for an ending activity.

Middle

Pass out *Activity Page 20.* Read aloud the message at the top of the page. Then draw the children's attention to the pictures on Activity Page 19. Ask the children to cut out only the pictures of the people they can trust. Arrange the pictures on construction paper and glue in place.

End

Gather the children in a circle on the floor and teach them the following song:

🎵 **I Am Growing** *(To the tune of "Mary Had a Little Lamb")*

I am growing every day,
Every day,
Every day.
I am growing every day,
And I belong to God.

I am learning whom to trust,
Whom to trust,
Whom to trust.
I am learning whom to trust,
And all the safety rules.

I am a waitress in a restaurant.

Show the children the pictures taken earlier in this lesson. Help the children attach each picture to a piece of construction paper. Encourage the children to tell you what they were doing in the picture and write this under the picture. Put these pages with the other saved scrapbook pages.

Gather the children around the prayer table and lead them in the prayer found at the bottom of *Activity Page 20.* Conclude by singing the "I Am Growing" song.

Extra! Extra!

Thank-You Cards

Help the children make postcards to thank their community helpers. Give each child a 4" by 6" piece of tagboard. On one side write the words *Thank you for helping me.* Show the children how to make hearts using two thumbprints. Help the children place thumbprint hearts in the corners of the card on the side with the writing. Then help the children write their names at the bottom of the cards. Encourage the children to give these thank-you notes to people in their community who have helped them.

Thank you
for helping me.
Liz

Materials for Part 3:
- *Read to Me Page 21*
- a pan of water; dishwashing soap; a small toy boat
- white construction paper or drawing paper

Trusting Friends
(Part 3)

Theme: To help the children learn whom to trust.

Purpose:
• to discuss with the children situations when trusting or not trusting is essential.

Beginning

As the children enter the room, have Sudie Squirrel welcome them. Then help the children find the leaves with their names on them and place them on the tree.

Gather the children in a circle or group. Talk with the children about trusting others. Remind the children that there are people they can trust and people they cannot. Remind the children that we can always trust God.

Show the children the Bible. Tell them that in this book there is a story about trusting. Read from a children's Bible or tell in your own words the story of Jesus calming the storm (Luke 8:22–25). Explain that the apostles needed to trust Jesus. Jesus keeps us safe from harm.

Act out this story using props. In a pan of water, put a small amount of dish soap. Then float a toy boat. Let the children blow through straws into the water to make rough seas as you re-tell the story.

Middle

Pass out a copy of *Read to Me Page 21* to each child. Invite the children to look at the illustrations as you read the story to the children. After reading the story, ask the children when it is all right to talk to a stranger (*if they ask a grown-up they trust first*).

End

Begin a book of Bible stories for the children. For each child, fold several sheets of white paper in half and staple along the folded edge to make a book. Write on the cover page the words *My Book of Bible Stories* and the child's name. Help the children complete the first page in their booklets by having them illustrate Jesus calming the rough seas. Let children fingerpaint blue to make water on the bottom of the page. Sponge an oval on top of the water for the boat. Using fingers dipped in a stamp pad, have the children add fingerprints for faces of the apostles in the boat. Cut a popsicle stick in half and attach both halves coming out of the boat as oars. Write the words *Jesus Calms the Storm* across the top of each child's page.

Jesus calms the storm.

Gather the children around the prayer table and lead them in the following prayer: "Dear God, thank you for always taking care of us. Amen."

Extra! Extra!

Floating Boats

Prepare a snack to go along with the Bible story of Jesus calming the storm. Give each child a small cup of blue gelatin. Let the children add whipped cream waves. Have them "float" an oval cookie on top of the waves. Put candy-coated chocolates on the cookie for the people on the boat. Add two pretzel sticks for oars. Eat and enjoy. *Note: Be aware of any children with food allergies before using this activity.*

Read page 12 of the book *God's Paintbrush* by Sandy Sasso Eisenberg. Ask the children to imagine what God's lap looks like. How would you feel sitting on God's lap?

Materials for Lesson 6, Part 1:

- *Activity Page 23*
- a suitcase with props such as a witch's hat, ballerina's shoes, a football player's helmet, a ghost costume

Theme: Halloween is a celebration that allows us to share the gift of imagination with others.

Purpose:
• *to affirm the children's delight in celebrating Halloween while reviewing rules for their safety.*

Beginning
Before the children come into the kindergarten room, put a mask or costume on Sudie Squirrel.

As the children enter the room, have Sudie Squirrel welcome them. Then help the children find the leaves with their names on them and place them on the tree.

Decorate the room with Halloween symbols. Fill a suitcase with an assortment of costume props such as a cowboy hat, a ballerina's shoes, a football player's helmet, and a ghost costume.

Gather the children in a circle and tell them that a special day is coming: Halloween! Halloween means the evening before All Saints' Day, which we'll talk about later. Explain that on Halloween we get to dress up and play make-believe. Tell the children that we are going to take a magic carpet ride to some make-believe places. Then pull out a prop (such as the cowboy hat) from the suitcase and say:

"Magic Carpet, take us today,
To a land that's far, far away
Where cowboys ride with hats so tall.
Take us, Magic Carpet, one and all."

Then pretend to go on a magic carpet ride to a ranch (dance recital, football game, haunted house). Encourage the children to pretend that they are cowboys and cowgirls. How would they act? What would they wear? Eat?

For the ballerina shoes, substitute "Where ballerinas on their toes stand tall" for the third line in the poem. For the football helmet, substitute "Where a football player scores with a ball" for the third line in the poem. For the ghost costume, substitute "Where ghosts fly through the night and call" for the third line in the poem.

Middle
Pass out a copy of *Activity Page 23* to each child. Read the paragraph at the top of the page. Help the children complete the Halloween safety quiz. Read each question and ask for volunteers to answer. Discuss each rule with the children.

End
Teach the children the following fingerplay:

Pumpkin, Pumpkin
Pumpkin, pumpkin, God made you (*Extend arms in big circle.*)
Big and fat and round. (*Shake arms side to side.*)
I'm glad you smile on Halloween (*Point to smile.*)
And never make a sound. (*Put finger to lips for silence.*)
Your face is always cheery, (*Open hands at side of face.*)
With mouth and eyes and nose. (*Point to mouth, eyes, nose.*)
With a bright and shiny candle (*Put index finger straight up.*)
See how my pumpkin glows! (*Open and close hands quickly.*)

Gather the children around the prayer table and lead them in the following prayer: "Dear God, thank you for the fun we have at Halloween! Amen."

Extra! Extra!

 Treat Bags

Provide a large brown paper bag for each child. Give the children sponges cut into pumpkin shapes. Provide plates of orange paint for the children to dip the sponges in. Encourage the children to print several pumpkins on their bags.

A People Graph

Use the props from the beginning of this lesson. Place each one on the floor at the front of the room. Then ask the children which of these would they most like to be dressed up as for Halloween. Have the children sit in a row next to their choices, making a people graph.

Materials for Part 2:
- *Activity Page 24*
- pumpkin
- carving tool
- candle or small flashlight
- air-dry clay
- orange markers
- birthday candles
- sugar cookies
- orange icing
- candy corn and licorice whips
- orange punch
- six small water bottles spray painted white
- black permanent marker

Halloween and All Saints' Day (Part 2)

Theme: God wants us all to be happy and safe.

Purpose:

• *to help the children enter into the fun of the Halloween celebration.*

Beginning

As the children enter the room, have Sudie Squirrel welcome them. Then help the children find the leaves with their names on them and place them on the tree.

Gather the children in a circle around a table. Tell the children that for a long, long time people have been celebrating Halloween. It occurs during the fall season when God's gifts of fruits and vegetables are plentiful. Point out that the pumpkin, which is harvested in the fall, is part of our Halloween fun. Explain that people use pumpkins to make jack-o'-lanterns as part of their Halloween fun.

Have a real pumpkin in the room. Help the children decide on a face to carve. As the children look on, carve the pumpkin, saving the seeds for roasting. Let the children look, feel, and smell inside the pumpkin.

Place a small candle inside the jack-o'-lantern. Light this candle and turn off the lights in the room. Explain that jack-o'-lanterns are used to give light on Halloween. Note: If fire laws forbid candles, use a small flashlight.

Middle

Pass out a copy of *Activity Page 24* to each child. Explain that three children are going trick-or-treating in their neighborhood. Point out that an adult is with them. Ask the children to help the group have a happy, safe journey home. Encourage the children to name things the group will pass on the way home. Then invite the children to use a crayon to help the group follow the correct path home.

End

Celebrate Halloween by setting up three centers around the room. In the first center, have the children make a pumpkin candle holder. Give each child a piece of air-dry clay and have him or her shape it into a ball. Have the children use markers to color this clay orange to resemble a pumpkin. Insert a birthday candle in the top of the pumpkin to make a candle holder.

The second center should be a treat center. Have the children spread orange icing on round sugar cookies. Provide candy corn and licorice whips to make the cookies look like jack-o'-lanterns. Provide orange punch or fruit drink for the children to enjoy. *Note: Be aware of any children with food allergies before using this activity.*

In the third center, set up a "ghostly bowling" game. Ahead of time spray paint six small plastic water bottles white. Draw two ovals for eyes with a black permanent marker on each bottle so they resemble ghosts. Line the six bottles up in a triangle. Let children take turns rolling a ball, trying to knock down as many ghosts as they can.

Gather the children around the prayer table and lead them in the following prayer: "Dear God, thank you for the gift of Halloween. Amen."

Extra! Extra!

Teach the children the following song. Once the children have learned the words, add motions to act it out.

♫ Halloween Fun
(To the tune of "The Mulberry Bush")

Pumpkins grow on a vine,
On a vine, on a vine.
Pumpkins grow on a vine
At Halloween time.

Pumpkins grow orange and round,
Orange and round, orange and round.
Pumpkins grow orange and round
At Halloween time.

This is the way we pick the pumpkin,
Pick the pumpkin, pick the pumpkin.
This is the way we pick the pumpkin
At Halloween time.

This is the way we scoop the seeds,
Scoop the seeds, scoop the seeds.
This is the way we scoop the seeds
At Halloween time.

This is the way we carve a face,
Carve a face, carve a face.
This is the way we carve a face
At Halloween time.

We light the candle and let it shine,
Let it shine, let it shine.
We light the candle and let it shine
At Halloween time.

We dress in costume and trick-or-treat,
Trick-or-treat, trick-or-treat.
We dress in costume and trick-or-treat
At Halloween time.

Materials for Part 3:
- *Read to Me Page 25*
- a wall calendar

Halloween and All Saints' Day (Part 3)

Theme: All Saints' Day is a special day when we honor very holy people who belong to God.

Purpose:
• *to introduce the feast of All Saints' Day.*

Beginning

As the children enter the room, have Sudie Squirrel welcome them. Then help the children find the leaves with their names on them and place them on the tree.

Show the children a calendar. Point to October 31. Tell them this is Halloween, a favorite celebration. Then turn the calendar over and point to November 1. Tell the children that the day after Halloween, November 1, is one of our favorite celebrations in the Catholic Church. A long time ago the Catholic Church decided to celebrate November 1 as the day to honor the people we call saints. Saints are very good people who loved God best of all. We believe the saints are in heaven with God forever.

Middle

Pass out a copy of *Read to Me Page 25* to each child. Read aloud the story of All Saints' Day. Ask the children to listen to try to answer the question, "What is a saint?" After you finish reading the story, ask the questions on the page.

Point out that although the Church leaders set one day aside each year to honor all the saints together, there are also certain days of the year to honor individual saints.

End

Tell the children a little bit about the saints pictured on *Read to Me Page 25.* Encourage the children to look at the pictures of the saints as you tell the children about each one.

Saint Francis lived a simple and happy life. He taught people about Jesus. He set an example for all people to live in peace and harmony with all God's creatures.

Blessed Kateri Tekakwitha was a Native American of the Mohawk people in what is now New York State. She became a Christian against her family's wishes. She lived a life of devotion to Jesus by helping to take care of the sick, the helpless, and the poor. Someday the Catholic Church may recognize Blessed Kateri as a saint.

Saint Martin de Porres was a poor boy of Lima, Peru. He entered a Dominican monastery at the age of fifteen. He became a healer of the sick in the monastery and in the city. He cared about children and animals.

Saint Elizabeth Seton is our first American-born saint. She was devoted to helping children. She founded the first American community of sisters to teach and to care for children.

Saint Patrick is the patron saint of Ireland. He was born in Scotland and kidnapped and taken to Ireland as a young boy. After a few years, he was returned to his home in Scotland. Later, he returned to Ireland where, as priest and bishop, he used the shamrock to teach people about God—the Father, the Son, and the Holy Spirit.

Lead the children in the following prayer: "Thank you, God, for our holy saints. They loved you most of all. They worked so hard to spread your love to others. Help us to be like them. Amen."

Extra! Extra!

 A Saints Booklet

Give each child five pieces of paper, one for each of the saints presented in the lesson. Explain that we will make a page for each saint that will remind us of him or her.

For Saint Francis, have the children draw a picture of their favorite animals. Then write on the bottom of the page: *Saint Francis lived in harmony with all God's creatures.*

For Blessed Kateri Tekakwitha, have the children attach a bandage to the page. Then have the children trace around small circles and make coins. Write across the bottom of this page: *Blessed Kateri Tekakwitha took care of the sick, the helpless, and the poor.*

On the third page, have the children draw a picture of themselves. Then write: *Saint Martin de Porres cared about children like me.*

For Saint Elizabeth Seton, have the children trace around their hands with fingers closed and pointed sideways. Using markers, have the children make this hand look like an American flag. Write: *Saint Elizabeth Seton is the first American-born saint.*

The last page is about Saint Patrick. Have the children trace around a heart three times on green construction paper and cut these out. Show the children how to arrange these hearts with the points together to form a shamrock. Have the children use a crayon to add a stem. Write across the bottom of this page: *Saint Patrick, the patron saint of Ireland, used a shamrock to teach the people about God.*

Staple all the pages together. Encourage the children to bring these booklets home and tell their families about the saints.

 Read the book *Francis, the Poor Man of Assisi* by Tomie de Paola.

Materials for Lesson 7, Part 1:
- *Activity Page 27*
- fruits, vegetables, nuts, and so on
- long piece of brown paper
- yellow construction paper
- unpopped popcorn
- green construction paper

Thanksgiving Day

Theme: Thanksgiving Day is a special time to thank God for the gifts of the harvest.

Purpose:
• *to help the children appreciate God's gifts that come to us at the time of the harvest.*

Beginning
Before the children gather, make an attractive arrangement of some of the fruits, vegetables, nuts, and so on, that are available in your part of the country in the fall.

As the children enter the room, have Sudie Squirrel welcome them. Then help the children find the leaves with their names on them and place them on the tree.

Gather the children around the display. Call their attention to the various shapes, colors, smells, textures, and so on, of the harvest. Discuss these items, asking whether the children have ever seen these foods grown or harvested. If possible, allow the children to taste small bites of some of the varieties. Ask how these foods are enjoyed in their homes. Invite the children to tell about other foods they enjoy that are harvested in the fall. Discuss where these foods come from. (Most children think these foods come from the store, but do not have any idea how they get to the store.) Explain to the children that these foods are gifts from God. With God's help, these foods grow in many different ways. God gives us these foods so we can grow, too.

Explain to the children that on Thanksgiving Day we gather to give thanks for God's gifts of the harvest and the foods we enjoy every day. Tell the children that this holiday was started over two hundred years ago by some of the early settlers in America.

Middle
Pass out a copy of *Activity Page 27* to each child. Point out the large turkey at the top of the page. Remind the children that the turkey is the main symbol for the Thanksgiving holiday. Draw the children's attention to the pictures on the bottom of the page. Ask them to name the foods they see. Read aloud the first three lines on the page. Then invite the children to cut out the foods and paste them in the wagon. Ask the children to think of other foods to put in the wagon.

End
Begin a bulletin board of fall foods. Make a "garden" by attaching a long piece of brown paper to the wall. Help the children "plant corn" in this "garden" by tracing around each child's hand with fingers together on yellow construction paper and have the child cut this out. Help the child glue unpopped popcorn seeds to this. Attach strips of green construction paper for stalks and attach the corn to the top of the stalks. Trace around the children's hands with fingers together several times on green construction paper and cut out. Add these as leaves to the stalks. Explain to the children that we eat the seeds of the corn plant.

Gather the children around the prayer table and lead them in the following prayer: "Dear God, thank you for the food we eat each day. Amen."

Extra! Extra!

More Work in the Garden

Add to the "garden" bulletin board. Cut out several "bush" shapes from green construction paper and add them to the "garden." Have the children add cranberries to the bushes by dipping their fingers in red paint and making fingerprints on the "bushes."

Read *Oh, What a Thanksgiving!* by Steven Kroll.

Edible Cornucopias

Explain to the children that a cornucopia is a cone-shaped container filled with foods. It is used to symbolize the abundance of food that we are blessed with, especially at Thanksgiving time. Give each child one bugle-shaped corn chip. Fill with a dollop of white icing. Have fruit-shaped cereal or candies available. Show the children how to fill their cornucopias with these "fruits."

Note: Be aware of any children with food allergies before using this activity.

Materials for Part 2:
- *Activity Page 28*
- orange construction paper
- green construction paper
- green tissue paper

Thanksgiving Day (Part 2)

Theme: We remember that our food, our home, and our families are gifts from God.

Purpose:
• *to encourage children to share their families' customs at Thanksgiving and to see prayer as having an appropriate part in those celebrations.*

Beginning
As the children enter the room, have Sudie Squirrel welcome them. Then help the children find the leaves with their names on them and place them on the tree.

Gather the children in a circle on the floor. Tell the story of the first Thanksgiving to the children. Use props such as flannel board characters or puppets.

Teach the children the following song:

♫ Thanksgiving Song *(To the tune of "Away In a Manger")*

**Thanksgiving is coming
And we will give thanks,
Remembering the Pilgrims
Who sailed to our banks.**

**They worked and they planted.
They worshiped and prayed,
Rejoicing in blessings
And new friends they'd made.**

Middle
Pass out a copy of *Activity Page 28* to each child. Read aloud the first three lines. Ask the children how we let God know we are grateful for these gifts. Explain that one way is through prayer. Say the Thanksgiving Day Prayer for the children. Allow time for the children to color and decorate the prayer card. Have the children cut out the prayer card. Encourage the children to share it with their families on Thanksgiving Day.

End
Tell the children that like the Pilgrims, we will "plant" more food in our "garden." Explain that today we will add carrots and lettuce. Trace around each child's hand with fingers together on orange construction paper and have the children cut these out. Then trace around each child's hand with fingers apart on green construction paper and help the children cut these out. Attach the green handprint to the top of the orange handprint with fingers pointing away from each other to make a carrot. "Plant" this in the garden by attaching the orange part to the brown paper and having the green part extend above the brown paper. To "plant" lettuce in the garden, give each child a large piece of green tissue paper. Have them crumple this into a loose ball and attach to the top of the brown paper. Explain to the children that we eat the root part of a carrot plant and the leaves of the lettuce plant.

Gather the children around the prayer table with their prayer cards. Hold your copy of the prayer card for them to see. Read the prayer on the prayer cards, inviting the children to repeat each line after you read it. Keep the cards for Part 3.

54

Extra! Extra!

Paper Bag Cornncopia

Make a cornucopia from a large brown paper bag. Roll down the edges of the opening of the bag. Twist the bottom part of the bag to form the cone shape of the cornucopia. Let each child select one food from the display used in Part 1 of this lesson to place inside the cornucopia. Use this cornucopia for a centerpiece for the feast held in Part 3 of this lesson.

Read one of the following books to the children: *The Pilgrims' First Thanksgiving* by Ann McGovern or *The Thanksgiving Story* by Alice Dalgliesh.

Materials for Part 3:
- *Read to Me Page 29*
- large cardboard box
- long piece of newsprint or white paper
- cornucopia
- fruit slices, cheese cubes, turkey cubes, corn muffins, and juice
- Thankgiving Day prayer cards

Thanksgiving Day (Part 3)

Theme: We remember and celebrate the first Thanksgiving Day in America.

Purpose:

• *to begin a simple introduction to the origins of our country's first Thanksgiving Day.*

Beginning

As the children enter the room, have Sudie Squirrel welcome them. Then help the children find the leaves with their names on them and place them on the tree.

Review the story of the first Thanksgiving with the children. Encourage the children to act out the story of the first Thanksgiving, beginning with the Pilgrims' trip on the Mayflower. Provide a large cardboard box for the children to use as a boat. Encourage the children to imagine what it would feel like to be on a boat on the ocean for many days. How would they feel traveling to a new and unknown land? What would they think when they saw Native Americans for the first time? Help the children explore what might have happened when the Pilgrims first met the Native Americans. Continue with the reenactment until the first Thanksgiving feast.

Sing the "Thanksgiving Song" found on page 54 with the children.

Middle

Pass out a copy of *Read to Me Page 29* to each child. Direct the children's attention to the illustrations. Discuss who the people are and the other illustrations. Tell the children to listen to the story to try to find answers to the question of the ways we say "thank you" to God. Then read the story aloud. Each time you come to a drawing, let the children say as a group what or who it is. Point out that today we still need to help one another and to share our gifts. Ask how we say "thank you" to God. Encourage all to participate in the discussion.

End

Prepare and share a Thanksgiving celebration. Explain to the children that we will now share in a feast to give thanks to God for our friends in kindergarten. Roll out a long piece of newsprint or white paper on the ground to be used as a tablecloth. Place paper plates around the "cloth" and have the children sit on the ground with legs crossed. Place a cornucopia in the center of the "cloth." Provide foods such as fruit slices, cheese cubes, turkey cubes, corn muffins, and juice for the children to enjoy. Before eating, lead the children in saying the Thanksgiving Day Prayer from their prayer cards (from Part 2). *Note: Be aware of any children with food allergies before using this activity.*

Gather the children around the prayer table and lead them in the following prayer: "Thank you, dear God, for our families that love us, for the food that nourishes us, and for the homes that welcome us. Amen."

Extra! Extra!

Read *Arthur's Thanksgiving* by Marc Brown; *Clifford's Thanksgiving Visit* by Norman Bridwell; *Sarah Morton's Day: A Day in the Life of a Pilgrim Girl,* by Kate Waters; or *Samuel Eaton's Day: A Day in the Life of a Pilgrim Boy* by Kate Waters.

Materials for Lesson 8, Part 1:
- *Activity Page 31*
- several books, including the Bible
- saltine crackers and cream cheese
- celery or carrot sticks

Theme: The Bible is God's holy word.

Purpose:
• *to teach the children respect for the Bible.*

Beginning

As the children enter the room, have Sudie Squirrel welcome them. Then help the children find the leaves with their names on them and place them on the tree.

Gather the children in a circle on the floor. Have several books, including some that you have already read, on display. Be sure to include the Bible. Show the children the books. Tell them that one of these books is very special. Show them the Bible. Explain that the Bible is God's holy book. In the Bible we read that God made us and loves us all.

Teach the children the following song:

♫ The Bible *(To the tune of "London Bridge")*

**The Bible is God's holy book,
God's holy book,
God's holy book.
The Bible is God's holy book.
Let's read a Bible story.**

Middle

Pass out a copy of *Activity Page 31* to the children. Point to the book at the top of the page. Ask whether any of the children know what book this is. Explain that this is the Bible. Read aloud the message at the top of the page. Call attention to the special space which looks very much like our prayer table where we keep our Bible in the kindergarten room. Encourage the children to make the special place on their pages a beautiful place by adding a flame to the candle, coloring in the cross, and drawing flowers in the vase. Provide markers and crayons for the children to use.

End

Make a "Bible Book Snack" to enjoy. Give each child two saltine crackers and have them place these next to each other on a plate. Help the children spread cream cheese on both these crackers to make "pages" in the open Bible. Give each child a thin celery or carrot stick to place across the pages as a book mark. Let the children eat and enjoy. *Note: Be aware of any children with food allergies before using this activity.*

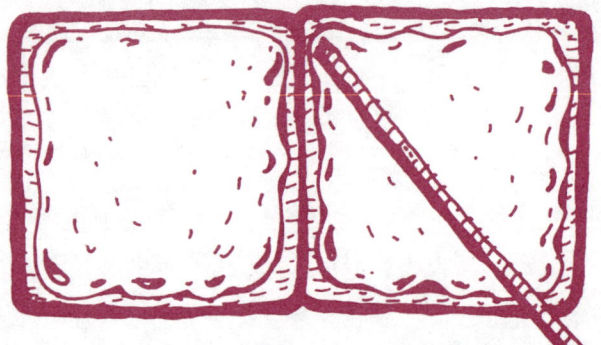

Gather the children around the prayer table and lead them in the following prayer: "Dear God, thank you for giving us your special book, the Bible. Amen."

Extra! Extra!

A Special Book Cover

Help the children make a cover for their Bible story books. Give each child a piece of colored construction paper folded in half. Draw a cross on the outside of this paper. Have the children fill in this cross with glue and then tear colored paper into small pieces and place them on the glue. Encourage the children to completely fill in the cross to make a mosaic. When finished, staple these covers to the children's Bible story booklets.

Materials for Part 2:
- *Activity Page 32*
- a Bible
- empty pitcher or jug
- pitcher or jug filled with grape juice or apple juice
- tagboard
- sticky velcro
- carpet square

The Bible
(Part 2)

Theme: The Bible teaches us about God's goodness.

Purpose:
• *to help the children appreciate that the Bible tells us about Jesus, the Son of God.*

Beginning

As the children enter the room, have Sudie Squirrel welcome them. Then help the children find the leaves with their names on them and place them on the tree.

Gather the children in a circle on the floor. Show them the Bible and ask whether they can remember the name of this special book. Remind them that this book tells us about God's only Son, Jesus. Tell them that today, we will read a story from this book. It is a story about Jesus and his mother Mary. In this story, Jesus performs his first miracle. Read from a children's Bible or tell in your own words the story of the wedding at Cana (John 2:1–11). As you tell or read the story, show the children an empty pitcher or jug and explain that this was similar to what was at the wedding. Fill the pitcher with water (from a gallon jug of water or sink). Then explain to the children that Jesus changed the water

into wine. Remind the children that only God performs miracles. If we want to make this water into another drink we have to add something like apple or grape juice. Mix the drink and pour each child a small cup of the juice from the pitcher.

To enhance the experience, prepare pictures from the story on tagboard, color, and cut out. Attach a piece of sticky velcro to the back and put on a carpet square as you tell or read the story, or use Sadlier's *Bible Felt Art Kit*.

Middle
Pass out a copy of *Activity Page 32* to each child. Read the paragraph at the top of the page. Then draw the children's attention to the picture of Jesus and the children. Invite the children to color the picture and then cut it out. Have the children bring this picture home to put in a special place.

End
Using the tagboard or flannel board figures, invite volunteers to come and re-tell the story of the wedding at Cana. Then have children illustrate this story in their Bible booklets. Write the words *Wedding at Cana, Jesus' First Miracle* across the bottom of the page for each child.

Gather the children around the prayer table and lead them in singing the song, "The Bible" on page 58. Remind the children that songs can be offered as prayers.

Extra! Extra!

A Special Jug

Help the children make a wine jug like the one in the story of the wedding at Cana. Give each child an empty film container and some air-dry clay. Have the children mold the air-dry clay around the film container to make a jug-like container. Show the children how to roll two small pieces of clay into "snakes" and attach these to the jug as handles. Allow to dry. Encourage the children to take these home and use them to tell the story they just learned to their families.

Materials for Part 3:

- the Bible
- a children's Bible
- tagboard pictures or Sadlier's *Bible Felt Art Kit*
- sticky velcro
- carpet square
- masking tape
- real fishing nets
- plastic or construction paper fish

The Bible
(Part 3)

Theme: We come to know Jesus from stories in the Bible.

Purpose:
• to help the children appreciate that in the Bible we read about Jesus, the Son of God.

Beginning

As the children enter the room, have Sudie Squirrel welcome them. Then help the children find the leaves with their names on them and place them on the tree.

Gather the children in a circle on the floor. Show them the Bible. Tell the children that we will hear another story from this book. Read from a children's Bible or tell in your own words the story of the catch of fishes (Luke 5:1–11).

To enhance the experience, prepare pictures from the story on tagboard, color and cut out. Attach a piece of sticky velcro to the back and put on a carpet square as you tell or read the story, or use Sadlier's *Bible Felt Art Kit* characters.

After telling the story, have the children act it out. Put masking tape on the floor in the outline of a boat. Have several children sit "inside" this boat. Provide real nets (the ones with handles on them will do) for the children to use. Have these children pretend to be fishing from one side of the boat, not catching anything. Then have another child play the part of Jesus and tell the children to put their nets

on the other side of the boat. When the children do this, have someone fill the nets with plastic or construction paper fish.

Middle

Invite volunteers to use the tagboard or flannel board characters and re-tell the story of the catch of fishes. Then have the children illustrate this story in their Bible booklets. Write *The Catch of Fishes* across the top of each child's page.

End

To conclude this unit, take down all the fall decorations around the room. Give the children the leaves with their names on them to take home. Explain to the children that, when they come back to school, we will have something new with their names on them to hang on our tree.

Gather around the prayer table and say the following prayer with the children: "Dear God, thank you for giving us the Bible so we may learn about your Son, Jesus. Amen."

Extra! Extra!

Full Nets

Make edible fish nets for the children to eat. Give each child a paper plate and some licorice whip. Show the children how to cut pieces of licorice whip and lay them across their plates all in the same direction. Then have the children cut more pieces of licorice whip and lay these across the first set to form a net. Put goldfish crackers in the "nets" and let the children enjoy their catches. *Note: Be aware of any children with food allergies before using this activity.*

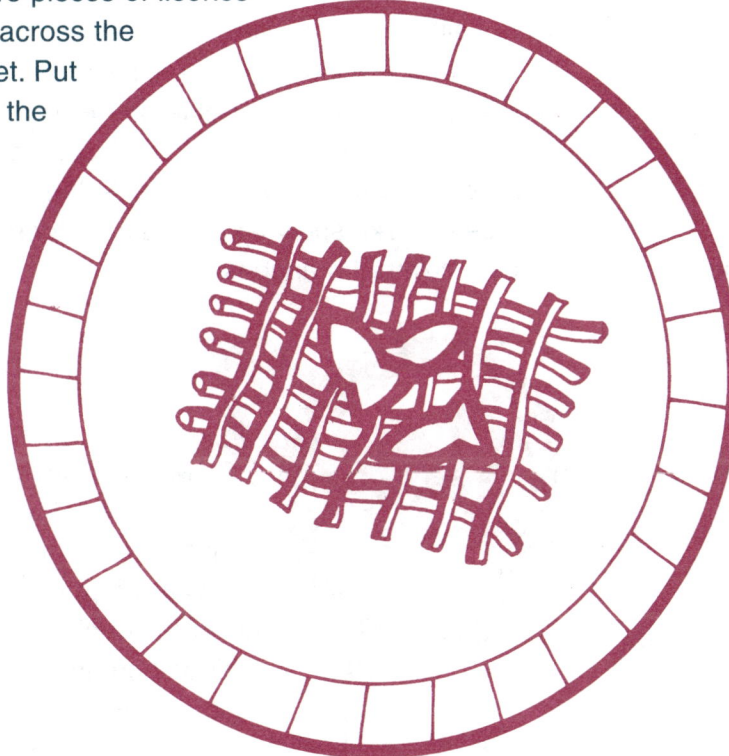

Materials for *Winter Unit Page*:

- *Unit Page 33*
- snowflakes
- mittens, caps, coats, scarves, rubber boots, ice skates and so on
- empty paper towel spools
- brown paint
- white tissue paper
- sugar cookies
- whipped cream
- sugar
- chocolate-covered cookie sticks
- hot chocolate

Unit 2
Wonderfully Made by God

Theme: Celebrating Winter

Beginning

A small tree should be attached to the wall at the children's eye level. Prepare a snowflake from white construction paper for each child with his or her name on it. As each child enters the kindergarten room, he or she should find the snowflake with his or her name on it and attach it to the tree.

Introduce the season of winter by bringing in items that are particular to this time of year. Some items might include mittens, caps, coats, scarves, rubber boots, ice skates, hockey sticks, and hot chocolate. Gather the children and show them these objects. Talk about the season of winter. Explain that in winter, the leaves that have turned colors have all fallen off the trees and the weather starts to get even colder.

Teach the children the following song:

♫ **Winter's Here** *(To the tune of "Frère Jacques")*

**Winter's here, winter's here.
White snowflakes, white snowflakes;
Mittens and hot chocolate, mittens and hot chocolate;
Celebrate! Celebrate!**

Middle

Pass out a copy of the *Unit Page* to each child. Explain that the pictures show people having fun doing things in winter. Invite the children to make up a story about each picture. Ask the children what they like to do in winter.

End

Make "A Snowy Day Tree." Give each child an empty paper towel spool. Have the children paint this brown. Cut several slits in the top and bend the strips outward to form branches. Have the children put a thin layer of glue on these branches. Give the children white tissue paper squares. Show them how to crumple the tissue squares to make snowflakes and stick them onto the glue-covered branches.

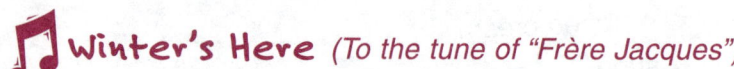

Make "Wonderful Winter Trees" together. Give each child a round sugar cookie. Have the children cover this with whipped cream. Then have the children sprinkle sparkly sugar on the whipped cream. Give each child a rectangular chocolate-covered cookie stick to use as a tree trunk. Enjoy with hot chocolate. *Note: Be aware of any children with food allergies before using this activity.*

Extra! Extra!

 A Handprint Winter Tree

Paint each child's forearm brown (the tree-trunk) and stamp this onto a piece of light blue construction paper. Paint the child's hand (with fingers open wide) brown. Help the child stamp this at the top of the trunk to complete the tree. White paint may be sponged on to add snow to the tree branches.

 Read any of the following books:

Snowballs, by Lois Eklert, published by Harcourt Brace & Company, (San Diego, CA) 1995.

The Big Snow, by Berta and Elmer Hader, published by Simon & Schuster Books for Young Readers, (New York) 1976.

When Winter Comes, by Robert Maass, published by Henry Holt and Company, Inc., (New York) 1996.

The Hat, by Jan Brett, published by The Putnam Publishing Group, (New York) 1997.

The Jacket I Wear in the Snow, by Shirley Neitzel, published by William Morrow & Company, (New York) 1994.

The Mitten, by Jan Brett, published by The Putnam Publishing Group, (New York) 1996.

The Snowy Day, by Ezra Jack Keats, published by Viking Children's Books, (New York) 1998.

Additional Suggestions for Storytime During Unit 2

Berenstain, Jan and Stan. *Berenstain Bears and the Week at Grandma's.* New York: Random House, Inc., 1986.

Buckley, Helen E. *Grandfather and I.* New York: Lothrop, Lee & Shepherd Books, 1994.

Carle, Eric. *Let's Paint a Rainbow.* New York: Scholastic, Inc., 1998.

dePaola, Tomie. *First Christmas.* New York: Putnam Publishing Group, 1984.

_____. *The Friendly Beasts, An Old English Christmas Carol.* New York: Putnam Publishing Group, 1998.

Dunbar, Joyce. *This Is the Star.* San Diego, CA: Harcourt Brace & Co., 1998.

Everitt, Betsy. *Mean Soup.* San Diego, CA: Harcourt Brace & Company, 1995.

Hennessy, B.G. *The First Night.* New York: Viking Children's Books, 1993.

Hoffman, Mary. *Amazing Grace.* New York: Scholastic, Inc., 1991.

Keats, Ezra Jack. *The Little Drummer Boy.* New York: Simon & Schuster Children's Book, 1972.

Lucado, Max. *Jacob's Gift.* Nashville, TN: Thomas Nelso Inc., 1998.

Pfister, Marcus. *The Christmas Star.* New York: North-South Books, 1993.

Slate, Joseph. *Who Is Coming to Our House?* New York: The Putnam Publishing Group, 1996.

Wilde, Oscar. *The Selfish Giant.* New York: The Putnam Publishing Group, 1995.

Wildsmith, Brian. *Creation.* Brookfield CT: Millbrook Press, 1996.

 **Materials for Lesson 9, Part 1:**

- *Activity Page 35*
- pictures of the sun, stars, water, plants, animals, people
- tagboard
- stick velcro
- carpet square

Theme: We thank God for the gift of living things.

Purpose:
- *to help the children explore the wonders of creation in both living and non-living things.*

Beginning

As the children enter the room, have Sudie Squirrel welcome them. Then help the children find the snowflakes with their names on them and place them on the tree.

Gather the children around you. Talk about the living things in our world. Include in this discussion people, animals, fish, birds, trees, and flowers. If possible, take the children for a walk outside or look out a window to see some other living things. You may want to show the children pictures of a variety of living things throughout the world. Explain some ways we experience living things and benefit from them.

Teach the children the following song:

🎵 God's Great Big World (To the tune of "London Bridge")

God gave us our great big world,
Great big world,
Great big world.
God gave us our great big world.
God, we thank you.

Children all around the world,
'Round the world,
'Round the world,
Children all around the world:
God, we thank you.

Middle
Pass out a copy of *Activity Page 35* to each child. Read the top of the page to the group. Have the children look at the outdoor scene showing many living things God has created. Ask the children how we can know whether something is alive. Ask how many living things they can find. Have the children color all the things that are alive.

End
Ahead of time prepare pictures of the sun, stars, water, plants, animals, people, and so on from the creation story. Draw or mount these on tagboard and cut out. Color, laminate for durability, and attach a piece of sticky velcro to the back. Use a carpet remnant or square as the background.

Gather the children in a circle around you. Show the children the Bible. Tell them that the story of creation is in this special book. Use the pictures prepared earlier to tell the children that God made all these living things in our world. Have the children illustrate the things that God made for them in their Bible booklets. Write across each child's page the word *Creation.*

Gather the children around the prayer table and lead them in the following prayer: "Dear God, thank you for all your gifts of creation. Amen."

Extra! Extra!

 Read the book *Creation* by Brian Wildsmith.

Materials for Part 2:
- *Activity Page 36*
- round sugar cookies
- blue icing
- green sugar
- small heart candies

Our Wonderful World (Part 2)

Theme: We are able to help care for God's world.

Purpose:

• *to help the children experience and care for all of creation as a gift to us from God.*

Beginning

Before the children enter the room, make a mess of the toys, put trash on the floor, and have the chairs in disarray.

As the children enter the room, have Sudie Squirrel welcome them. Then help the children find the snowflakes with their names on them and place them on the tree.

Gather the children in a circle on the floor. Tell the children that Sudie was very upset when she came to kindergarten today. Tell the children to look what has happened to our room. Ask the children what we should do about it. Lead the children to the conclusion that we should clean up the mess and always take care of our room and our world so it never looks like this. Invite the children to help you clean up and put things back in order.

Middle

Pass out a copy of *Activity Page 36* to the children. Read the first paragraph to the group. Call the children's attention to the illustrations on the bottom of the page and on the side. Tell the children they are going to show how they can care for our world. Help the children cut out the pictures on the bottom of the page

and glue them where they belong. Read the biblical quote at the bottom of the page. Remind the children that everything God made is good.

End

Let the children enjoy a "Worldly Snack." Give each child a round sugar cookie. Show the children how to spread blue icing (for water) on the cookies. Give the children green sugar to sprinkle on the cookies for land. Put a small heart candy on the world to remind us to take care of the world that God gave us. Eat and enjoy. *Note: Be aware of any children with food allergies before using this activity.*

Gather the children around the prayer table and lead them in the following prayer: "Dear God, thank you for making the world and everything in it. Help us always to take good care of your wonderful gifts. Amen."

Extra! Extra!

 ## World Class Bags

Provide a brown paper bag for each child. Help the children sponge a large blue circle on one side of the bag. Have the children paint green on the blue, using a paint brush, to make the world. Then have the children sponge paint hearts on the other side of the bag. Encourage the children to bring these bags home and use them when needed for recycling or trash.

Materials for Part 3:
- *Read to Me Page 37*
- a large bowl
- water
- clay
- popsicle sticks
- tissue paper
- plastic fish, animals, and people

Our Wonderful World
(Part 3)

Theme: God made all living things.

Purpose:
- *to help the children appreciate God's gifts of all living things.*

Beginning

As the children enter the room, have Sudie Squirrel welcome them. Then help the children find the snowflakes with their names on them and place them on the tree.

Gather the children in a group around the table. Turn the lights off in the room. On the table, place a large bowl. Tell the children that God made everything. To celebrate God's creation we will make a miniature world. Follow the steps below:

- Pour a small amount of water into the bowl.
- Put clay in the bowl for earth and stick trees made from popsicle sticks and tissue paper into the clay.
- Have the children hold up cut-outs of the sun, moon and stars.
- Float plastic fish in the water in the bowl.
- Add plastic animals and people to the clay in the bowl.

Middle

Pass out a copy of the *Read to Me Page 37* to the children. Draw the children's attention to the illustrations. Tell the children you are going to read them a story about life on a farm and that what makes this story so unique is that it is really a poem. Ask the children, "Who made all living things?" Then read the entire poem. Discuss each stanza with the children, pointing out all the living things we see and hear on the farm.

End

Gather the children in a circle on the floor. Teach them the following song:

 **God Made Everything** *(To the tune of "Twinkle, Twinkle, Little Star")*

God made the earth and God made the sky.
God made the fish and the birds that fly.
Animals, flowers, trees so tall,
God made everything, great and small.
God made all the things I see.
God made you and God made me.

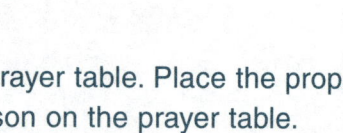

Gather the children around the prayer table. Place the props used in the beginning of this lesson on the prayer table. Lead the children in the following prayer: "Dear God, thank you for the gift of the world. Amen."

Extra! Extra!

 **A Small World**

Give each child a paper plate. Have the children spread prepared whipped topping (with blue food coloring added) on the bottom half of their plates for water. Give each child a vanilla wafer cookie to place at the top of his or her plate for the sun. To make land, have the children crush graham crackers in zippered plastic bags and sprinkle this along the top of the "water." Have the children make trees by adding pieces of green fruit roll-ups to pretzel sticks. Tell the children to place these on the land. Animal crackers can be added to the land as well. To make flowers, have the children place rainbow-colored fruit flavored candies on the crushed graham crackers. Tell the children that God created people, too—the ones who will now eat this lovely "creation." *Note: Be aware of any children with food allergies before using this activity.*

Materials for Lesson 10, Part 1:
- *Activity Page 39*
- a pretend microphone
- craft foam
- yarn or string
- glitter glue
- an instant camera

Theme: We are learning that we can do many things.

Purpose:
• *to help the children develop a strong self-image and a positive sense of self-worth by affirming their unique talents and abilities.*

Beginning
As the children enter the room, have Sudie Squirrel welcome them. Then help the children find the snowflakes with their names on them and place them on the tree.

Gather the children in a circle on the floor. Tell the children that today, we are going to celebrate all the wonderful things that they can do. Teach the children the following song:

♫ See What I Can Do *(To the tune of "The Farmer in the Dell")*

See what I can do,
See what I can do.
I can do so many things.
See what I can do.

Tell the children that each one of them will have a chance to show everyone something he or she can do. Use a pretend microphone or make one from an empty toilet paper spool with a ball of foil inserted in the top. Go around the circle and "interview" each child, asking them to tell you something they can do. Encourage every child to name something he or she can do, such as hop on one foot, ride a bike, walk backwards, and so on.

Have a "Celebration of the Stars." Let each child go to the middle of the circle and show what he or she can do. Applaud and sing the "See What I Can Do" song between performances.

Middle
Pass out a copy of *Activity Page 39* to each child. Call the children's attention to the pictures in the squares. Begin with the soccer game. Ask for volunteers to tell what the children are doing. Continue with the other pictures. Read the lines under the pictures and encourage the children to trace the words with their pencils. Then have the children draw a picture in the blank square of themselves doing something they can do well. Have them dictate to you what they are doing and write this under that picture.

End
Cut a star shape from craft foam for each child. Punch a hole through the top and thread a piece of yarn or string to make a necklace. Write each child's name on his or her star with a marker. Have the children use glitter glue to trace over their names and to outline the stars. When these have dried, have the children put the necklaces on and, using an instant camera, take a picture of each one. Keep the pictures for an activity in Part 2.

Gather the children around the prayer table and teach them the following prayer: "Dear God, thank you for making me so I can do many things. Amen."

Extra! Extra!

Read the book *This Is the Way* by Anne Dalton. As each page is read, ask the children whether they can do the things the children in the book are doing. Have different children act out the activities mentioned in the book.

Materials for Part 2:
- *Activity Page 40*
- a small broom, a dust cloth, a clothes hanger, a piece of chalk, a pair of scissors, a pencil, crayons
- box
- construction paper
- construction paper stars

See What I Can Do (Part 2)

Theme: People are the best part of all that God made.

Purpose:
• *to help the children appreciate that our abilities are gifts from God.*

Beginning
Ahead of time, gather some items that the children can use to show things they can do, such as a small broom, a dust cloth, a clothes hanger, a piece of chalk, a pair of scissors, a pencil, some crayons, and so on. Place all of these things in a box.

As the children enter the room, have Sudie Squirrel welcome them. Then help the children find the snowflakes with their names on them and place them on the tree.

Gather the children in a circle. Teach the children the following song:

♪ I Am Special (*To the tune of "If You're Happy and You Know It"*)

I am special and I know it, clap my hands. *(Clap hands.)*
I am special and I know it, clap my hands. *(Clap hands.)*
I am special and I know it,
And it's oh such fun to show it.
I am special and I know it, clap my hands. *(Clap hands.)*

Let me show you all the things that I can do. *(tap, tap)*
Let me show you all the things that I can do. *(tap, tap)*

I am special and I know it,
And it's oh such fun to show it.
Let me show you all the things that I can do. *(tap, tap)*

Pull out the box of items gathered earlier. Explain that this is our "Can Do Box." Tell the children that in this box are items that they can use to show some things they can do. Go around the circle and let each child have a turn to come up, select an item from the box, and show what he or she *can do*.

Middle
Pass out a copy of *Activity Page 40* to each child. Call the children's attention to the child at the top of the page. Ask the children to tell you what she is doing. Ask whether they have ever done that. Then read the first six lines on the top of the page. Have the children look at the pictures. Ask for volunteers to describe what is happening in each one. After the pictures have been discussed, encourage the children to trace the words under each picture. Read each sentence aloud. Then have the children cut out and fold where indicated to make a booklet.

End
Mount the pictures of the children taken in Part 1 of this lesson on pieces of construction paper. On each page, write the words *I Can* (*what the child did*) across the bottom. Let the children make borders by gluing construction paper stars around the pictures. Add this page to the children's scrapbooks.

Gather the children around the prayer table and lead them in the prayer found at the bottom of *Activity Page 40*.

74

Extra! Extra!

 Picture Me...

Help the children make picture frames to put a picture of themselves doing something in. Cut out a rectangular shape from black craft foam. Cut out the center of the rectangle to form a frame. Give each child a star pattern and some yellow craft foam. Have the children trace the pattern and cut out several stars from the craft foam. Help the children glue the stars around their frames. Then have the children glue glitter on these stars. When dry, the frames may be taken home.

Share the book *Things I Can Do Myself* by Craig John Lovic with the children.

 **Materials for Part 3:**
- *Read to Me Page 41*
- a cube with pictures of the five senses
- poster board
- velcro strips
- eyes, ears, nose, mouth, and hands
- bell
- treats
- lemon

See What I Can Do
(Part 3)

Theme: We use our senses to appreciate God's world.

Purpose:
• *to help the children appreciate our five senses that help us to enjoy the wonderful world God made for us.*

Beginning

As the children enter the room, have Sudie Squirrel welcome them. Then help the children find the snowflakes with their names on them and place them on the tree.

Gather the children in a circle on the floor. Tell the children that God has blessed us with the five senses: seeing, hearing, smelling, tasting, and touching. Talk with the children about what they can do with each sense.

Prepare a cube with pictures of the five senses on each side. (One sense should be used twice to fill the six sides.) Have one child roll the cube and name the sense that lands on top. Then ask each child to name something that he or she can taste, see, hear, smell, or touch, depending on the sense. Continue until each child has had a turn to roll the cube.

Middle

Pass out a copy of *Read to Me Page 41* to each child. Call the children's attention to the drawings on the right side of the page. Going from top to bottom, have the children say as a group what sense is pictured. Then have the children look at the other drawings on the page. As you point to each picture, ask the children which sense would they use to enjoy this. Then read the story of Alex aloud. When you have finished reading the story, ask the children whether they can tell you why Alex liked each of the things named. Ask the questions on the bottom of the page. Encourage all children to participate in the discussion. Remind the children that God gave us our five senses.

End

On a large poster, draw the outline of a face. Fill in hair. Put velcro strips where the eyes, ears, nose, and mouth should be. Put two more pieces of velcro right below the face for hands. Prepare eyes, ears, nose, mouth, and hands from poster board and attach velcro to each. As each sense is talked about, add the appropriate item until the poster is complete. Pass around a cut lemon. Ask the children what senses are needed to enjoy this lemon. (*smelling, seeing, touching*) Add the features to the poster for the senses mentioned. Ring a bell or play a musical note on an instrument. Ask the children which senses are needed to enjoy this. (*hearing*) Add the ears to the poster. Give each child a small treat. Ask the children which senses are needed to enjoy this. (*tasting, seeing, touching*) Add any remaining features that are not on the poster.

Gather the children around the prayer table and lead them in the following prayer: "Dear God, thank you for your wonderful gift of our senses. Amen."

Extra! Extra!

 Senses Booklet

Give each child a piece of paper with a nose drawn on it. Have them use their fingers pressed on a stamp pad to add nostrils on the nose. Show the children how to used brightly colored stamp pads to make fingerprint flowers right below the nose. Spray a small amount of perfume on the flowers. Write across the bottom of the page: *Smell.*

For page two of the booklet, put lipstick on each child's lips with a disposable cotton-tipped swab. Then have each child make a lip print by pressing their lips to a piece of paper. On this paper draw a spoon near the lips. Give the children several pictures of food cut from magazines to choose from and have them choose something they like the taste of. Have the children glue this picture to the spoon. Write across the bottom of the page: *Taste.*

On the next page of the senses booklet, have the children cut out and glue two white construction paper ovals (for eyes). Give the children small round sponges and different colors of paint. Have the children sponge paint the irises on their eyes the same color of their own eyes. Then show them how to press their fingers on a stamp pad and print small dots in the center of the irises. Write across the bottom of the page: *Sight.*

The fourth page should have *Hearing* written across the bottom of the page. Then have the children cut ear shapes from tan construction paper and glue these to the page. Have the children make fingerprints on this page using a stamp pad. Turn these fingerprints into notes using a black marker.

For the last page of the booklet, paint each child's hand and make a handprint on a piece of white construction paper. Have available small squares of fabric such as silk, velvet, burlap, terry cloth, and so on. When the handprints are dry, let the children select one fabric that they like to touch and have them glue this to the fingers of their handprints. Write across the bottom of the page: *Touch.*

Add a construction paper cover and staple the pages together. Write *My Book of Senses* across the front cover.

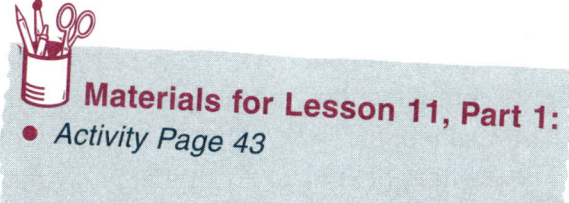

Materials for Lesson 11, Part 1:
- *Activity Page 43*

Theme: We are able to remember what we have learned.

Purpose:

• *to help the children recognize how many things they have learned and to imagine what they will soon be able to do.*

Beginning

As the children enter the room, have Sudie Squirrel welcome them. Then help the children find the snowflakes with their names on them and place them on the tree.

Gather the children around you. Remind them that, of all the wonderful things in God's world, people are God's greatest creation. We all have special talents, and we have the ability to discover, invent, remember, imagine, and pretend. Tell the children that we are going to play a "Remembering" game. Explain that this game helps them to develop their gift of memory, the ability to remember things. Ask them to raise their hands if they can remember an answer for questions you will ask. Ask questions such as, "What did you have for breakfast this morning?"; "Who brought you to school today?"; "What is the name of the person sitting next to you?"; "What is my name?" Encourage all children to participate.

Middle

Pass out a copy of *Activity Page 43* to the children. Read aloud each sentence of the "I Can" skills. Draw the children's attention to the illustrations. Have the children find which ones need to be completed. Encourage the children to complete each task as you read the sentences. Help as needed.

End

Gather the children around the table. Ask each child to tell something new he or she would like to learn to do. Some might be: bouncing a ball, tying shoes, dressing, or helping clean up. Then have the children draw a picture of themselves doing this new skill. Write on the children's papers what they are doing in the picture. Add this page to the children's scrapbooks.

Gather the children around the prayer table and lead them in the following prayer: "Dear God, thank you for making me. Help me to always learn new things. Amen."

Extra! Extra!

 Read the book *Amazing Grace* by Mary Hoffman. Explain to the children that Grace could do anything she put her mind to. Tell them that Grace used her imagination to pretend to be lots of different people.

Materials for Part 2:
- *Activity Page 44*

Learning New Things
(Part 2)

Theme: We remember that we are God's children.

Purpose:
• *to encourage the children to reflect on how much they have learned about God.*

Beginning

As the children enter the room, have Sudie Squirrel welcome them. Then help the children find the snowflakes with their names on them and place them on the tree.

Gather the children in a circle on the floor. Tell the children that they have learned many new things already this year. Remind them that they have learned many things about God. Teach them the following song:

♪ **I'm Learning About My God** *(To the tune of "Go 'Round the Village")*

I'm learning about my God.
I'm learning about my God.
I'm learning about my God.
I learn my God loves me.

I'm learning about my God.
I'm learning about my God.
I'm learning about my God,
My God who has made me.

I'm learning about my God.
I'm learning about my God.
I'm learning about my God,
My God who knows my name.

I'm learning about my God.
I'm learning about my God.
I'm learning about my God,
My God who made our world.

Middle
Pass out a copy of *Activity Page 44* to each child. Explain to the children that they will find some of the things they have learned about God on this page. Read aloud each sentence on the page. Explain to the children that a word in each sentence needs to be filled in by tracing the dots with their pencils. Read each sentence again and have the children trace the letters as you read.

End
Play "Look What I Can Do." Have the children stand in two lines facing each other. Explain that they are to try to do each of the things you say. Start with simple tasks so that all children will be successful. Some examples include:

• Touch your nose.
• Open your mouth.
• Clap your hands.
• Pat your head.
• Blink your eyes.
• Stamp your left foot.
• Hop on one foot.
• Touch your toes.

Gather the children around the prayer table and lead them in the prayer found at the bottom of *Activity Page 44*.

80

Extra! Extra!

Let's Go Exploring!

Review the story *Amazing Grace* with the children. Tell them that we will pretend to be explorers just like Grace did. Show the children the picture of Grace exploring for lost kingdoms. Ask the children what props we need to help our imaginations.

Have one empty paper towel roll available to use as a spy-glass. Invite the children to come up one at a time, look through the spy-glass, and describe the new place they have found.

♫ **An Activity Song**
(To the tune of "The Mulberry Bush")

**This is the way I touch my nose,
Touch my nose, touch my nose.
This is the way I touch my nose
So early in the morning.**

(Use the list of activities on page 80 as the basis for more verses.)

Materials for Part 3:
● *Read to Me Page 45*

Learning New Things (Part 3)

Theme: We are learning who Jesus is.

Purpose:

• to introduce Jesus to the children as God's own Son, the greatest of all God's gifts to us.

Beginning

As the children enter the room, have Sudie Squirrel welcome them. Then help the children find the snowflakes with their names on them and place them on the tree.

Gather the children in a circle on the floor. Remind the children that we are members of a special family, the Catholic Church. Teach the children the following song:

♪ I Am Growing *(To the tune of "Mary Had a Little Lamb")*

I am growing every day,
Every day,
Every day.
I am growing every day,
And I belong to God.

I am learning how to live,
How to live,
How to live.
I am learning how to live
As a child of God.

Middle

Pass out a copy of *Read to Me Page 45* to each child. Invite the children to look at the illustrations along the sides of the page. Have the children listen carefully as you read each section. Then ask the children what are some of the gifts that God gave us. And who is the greatest of all these gifts? Ask the three questions at the bottom of the page. Encourage all the children to participate in the discussion.

End

Remind the children that they are growing and learning new things every day. Then help them to make a group book entitled *I Am Growing*. Have the children divide their pages into three sections by folding them and then opening them back out. In the first section, have the children draw themselves as babies, doing something babies do, such as crawling or playing with a rattle. In the middle section of the page, have the children draw themselves doing something they can do now, such as playing ball. In the third section, have the children draw themselves doing something they cannot do now but hope to learn to do when they are older, such as ride a two-wheel bike or roller skate. Bind all the pages together into a book. Add a cover page with the title *I Am Growing* written on it. Leave this book out for the children to enjoy.

Gather the children around the prayer table and lead them in the following prayer: "Dear God, thank you for the gift of your Son, Jesus. Help me to grow in his love every day. Amen."

Extra! Extra!

Imagine This

Review the story *Amazing Grace* with the children. Tell them that we will pretend to be Aladdin just like Grace did. Show the children the picture of Grace pretending to be Aladdin in the book. Ask the children what props we need to help our imaginations. Provide a lamp or cut out of one. Let the children take turns "rubbing" the lamp and telling what they would wish for.

Materials for Lesson 12, Part 1:
- *Activity Page 47*
- three six-inch squares cut from a photo album page for each child
- masking tape
- green paint

Theme: Every day we grow and change.

Purpose:
• *to help the children be aware of the growth and changes in plants and animals.*

Beginning

As the children enter the room, have Sudie Squirrel welcome them. Then help the children find the snowflakes with their names on them and place them on the tree.

Gather the children in a circle. Tell the children that all living things go through different stages of growing and changing. Show the children photographs of a baby, a child, a teenager, a young adult, a middle-aged adult, and a very old adult. Hold up one picture at a time. Ask for volunteers to tell you what stage of development each person is in. Ask the children whether they have any friends or relatives in each of the stages of development.

Follow the same procedure with animals and plants. Then let the children act out the growth of a seed. Have the children crouch down into a ball for a seed. Then have them grow a little (put arms up). They continue growing (standing up more and more) until they are a full-grown "plant" (standing up tall with arms extended for leaves).

Middle

Pass out a copy of *Activity Page 47* to each child. Read the first two lines on the page. Then have the children look at the four pictures of corn growing. Ask the children to pick out the picture that shows the beginning of the plant and trace the number 1. Continue with help as needed.

End

Gather the children in a group around the table. Remind the children that all living things grow and change. Tell the children that we just talked about people growing and changing. Plants are living and so they grow and change. Help the children make a flip book of a plant growing. For each child, have three six-inch squares cut from photo album pages (the kind where the film can be lifted and photos inserted underneath). Remove the film from one square and help the child place one thumbprint near the bottom of the square. Explain that this is the seed of the plant. Replace the film over this thumbprint. Put a piece of masking tape on one edge to hold the film in place. Then help the children place a green print of his or her whole finger to make a stem coming from this seed on this film. Remove the piece of film from a second square and tape this on top of the other one. Have the children add a fingerprint bud on top of the stem and two green fingerprint leaves on the sides of the stem on this piece of film. Finally, add the film from the third square. Help the children add fingerprints to make petals around the bud to create a flower. To use the flip book, pull back all the film pages to reveal only the seed. Then replace one film page at a time, to show the plant growing a stem, then a bud and leaves, and finally a full grown flower.

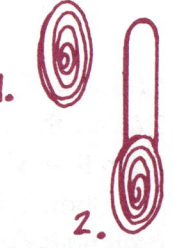

Gather the children around the prayer table. Lead them in the following prayer: "Dear God, thank you for being with me as I grow and change. Amen."

Extra! Extra!

How Does Your Garden Grow?

Provide the children with various kinds of seeds to explore. Let the children "play" with these seeds freely, noticing differences and similarities, grouping them, making patterns with them, or whatever they would like to do. Then give each child a piece of construction paper. Invite the children to make a picture using the seeds and gluing them onto the construction paper.

Materials for Part 2:
- *Activity Page 48*
- brown construction paper
- light blue construction paper
- green construction paper
- a current photo of each child

Growing and Changing (Part 2)

Theme: God wants us to grow and change.

Purpose:
• *to encourage the children's awareness of the human life cycle.*

Beginning

As the children enter the room, have Sudie Squirrel welcome them. Then help the children find the snowflakes with their names on them and place them on the tree.

Gather the children in a circle on the floor. If possible, bring pictures of yourself as a baby, a toddler, a teenager, and an adult. Talk about how you have grown and changed throughout the years. For example, point out that your feet, hands, legs, and arms are longer and bigger. Explain that while a person's body grows, a person's mind develops, too. We learn new things and our feelings about some things change. Even what we like to eat or to wear can change as we grow. Ask the children to name something they like to eat now but didn't like before. Ask whether they have toys they used to like but don't anymore.

Middle

Pass out a copy of *Activity Page 48* to each child. Read aloud the first paragraph at the top of the page. Ask the children to look at the illustrations. Explain that these are pictures of a boy growing from a baby to an older adult. Ask the children to number the pictures from 1 to 4, as they did with the plant. Then have the children cut the pictures out and punch holes in the top. Help them thread string or yarn through the holes and tie to a hanger or stick to make a mobile. Encourage the children to take these home and tell their families a story about people growing and changing.

End

Remind the children of the process of growing and changing of a plant from seed to flower. Then, on brown construction paper, trace around each child's foot with shoe on and cut out. Tell the children that this is a seed. Attach each child's baby picture to this "seed." Glue these seeds to a large pieces of light blue construction paper.

Trace around each child's forearm and hand with fingers closed on green construction paper and cut out. Glue these on the seeds on the blue construction paper.

Trace around each child's hand with fingers spread open on a colorful piece of construction paper and cut out. Put a current picture of the child in the center of this "flower" and attach to the stem on the blue construction paper. Add these pages to the children's scrapbooks.

Gather the children around the prayer table and lead them in the following prayer: "Dear God, help us to praise you in everything we say and do. Amen."

Extra! Extra!

Centering on the Stages of Life

Set up four centers around the room. In the first center, place items that babies would play with and use, such as rattles, blankets, bottles, diapers, and so on.

In the second center, put items that a child would play with or use, such as a ball, a puzzle, a hairbrush, books, and so on.

In the third center, place items that moms or dads would use, such as newspapers, computers, telephones, coffee cups, pots and pans, broom and cleaning supplies, books, golf clubs, and so on.

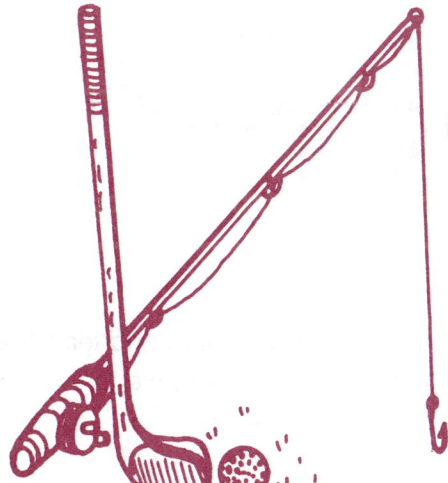

In the fourth center, place items that grandparents might use, such as fishing poles, golf clubs, books, sewing things, newspapers, mixing bowls and baking sheets, and so on.

Let the children move freely from center to center, pretending they are in that particular stage of life while in that center.

Materials for Part 3:
- *Read to Me Page 49*
- drawing paper

Growing and Changing (Part 3)

Theme: One day we will be with God in heaven.

Purpose:
• *to develop in the children an awareness of death as a part of God's plan for us.*

Beginning

As the children enter the room, have Sudie Squirrel welcome them. Then help the children find the snowflakes with their names on them and place them on the tree.

Gather the children in a circle on the floor. Tell the children that God knows each one of us by name. God knows when each of us was born. He knows what we are doing right now, as well as what we will be doing years from now. God has a plan for each of us. Teach the children the following song:

♪ **God Has a Plan** *(To the tune of "Mary Had a Little Lamb")*

God has got a plan for me,
Plan for me, plan for me.
God has got a plan for me.
I'm growing every day.

I'm growing in my family,
Family, family.
I'm growing in my family,
And in God's family, too.

Middle
Pass out a copy of the *Read to Me Page 49* to each child. Remind the children that God has a plan for all of us. Encourage the children to look at the illustrations as you read the story to the children.

End
Gather the children around the table. Ask them to share something special they do with an older adult like a grandparent or neighbor. (If there is no older adult that the child interacts with, have them share something they would like to do with a grandparent or older adult friend.) Then give each child a piece of paper and have them draw themselves doing this activity with the older adult. Write on their papers what they are doing and with whom. Save these pages for the children's scrapbooks.

I like to fish with Pop.

Gather the children around the prayer table and lead the children in the following prayer: "Dear God, we thank you for the gift of life. Help us to follow your plan. Amen."

Extra! Extra!

 Read the book *The Selfish Giant* by Oscar Wilde. Other books to share with the children include: *Berenstain Bears and the Week at Grandma's* by Jan and Stan Berenstain; *Grandfather and I* by Helen E. Buckley.

Materials for Lesson 13, Part 1:

- *Activity Page 51*
- shredded crinkled paper
- yellow, blue, and red crepe paper streamers
- paper plates
- whipped cream
- food coloring
- plastic spoons

Theme: We are learning what feelings are.

Purpose:
• *to enable the children to explore their experiences with feelings.*

Beginning

As the children enter the room, have Sudie Squirrel welcome them. Then help the children find the snowflakes with their names on them and place them on the tree.

Gather the children in a circle. Act out the following situations using Sudie Squirrel:

- Sudie was running down a tree and fell. Her paw was bleeding. How do you think Sudie felt?
- Sally Squirrel saw Sudie crying and came and helped her up. She put some medicine and a bandage on Sudie's paw. How do you think Sudie felt then?
- Sudie was working on a puzzle. She looked and looked and could not find the last piece. How do you think Sudie felt?
- Samuel helped Sudie find the piece. How do you think Sudie felt then?
- Momma Squirrel called Sudie to come have some fresh baked pecan pie and milk. How do you think Sudie felt?

Middle
Pass out a copy of *Activity Page 51* to each child. Call the children's attention to the puppet faces. Ask them how they think the puppets feel. How do they know? Tell the children to make the faces look like themselves and their friends. Give the children shredded crinkled paper to add for hair. Read the questions at the bottom of the page and encourage the children to share their experiences.

End
Gather the children around a table. Tell the children that we all have feelings. Explain that we can associate certain colors with different feelings. Show the children a yellow crepe paper streamer. Ask how the color yellow makes them feel. Tell the children that yellow is a happy color. Show the children a blue crepe paper streamer and explain that when people are sad, they often say they are feeling blue, so we associate the color blue with sad feelings. Show the children a red crepe paper streamer. Tell the children that red is often associated with the feeling of anger. Explain that we have all of these feelings and that is all right.

Give each child a paper plate with some whipped topping on it. Go around the group and ask each child whether they are feeling happy, sad or angry. Then add a few drops of food coloring to his or her whipped topping to help the child make the appropriate color. Encourage the children to mix the food color into the whipped topping with their fingers. Then give them spoons to enjoy their treats.

Note: Be aware of any children with food allergies before using this activity.

Gather the children around the prayer table and lead them in the following prayer: "Dear God, thank you for the gift of our feelings. Amen."

Extra! Extra!

A Feelings Stick

Use a large stick, broom handle, or yardstick. Let each child select a colored crepe paper streamer which shows how he or she is feeling. Attach all the streamers to the stick. Walk around the room waving the stick with the children following behind, ending up at the prayer table. Place the stick on the prayer table and say a prayer of thanks to God for all of our feelings.

Materials for Part 2:
- *Activity Page 52*
- red, blue, and yellow streamers
- poster board
- straws

I Have Feelings
(Part 2)

Theme: We are learning to deal with our feelings.

Purpose:
• to help the children understand that everyone has feelings and to learn appropriate ways to deal with our feelings.

Beginning
As the children enter the room, have Sudie Squirrel welcome them. Then help the children find the snowflakes with their names on them and place them on the tree.

Gather the children in a circle on the floor. Remind the children that we can associate colors with feelings. Review these for the children: yellow is associated with happy feelings, blue with sad feelings, and red with angry feelings.

Give each child three streamers, one of each color. As the children sing the following song, have them wave the appropriate color streamer.

♪ **Feelings** *(To the tune of "Sing a Song of Sixpence")*

Sometimes I feel happy. *(Make a happy face, wave yellow streamer.)*

And sometimes I feel sad. *(Make a sad face, wave blue streamer.)*

I can feel so angry, *(Make an angry face, wave red streamer.)*

And oh, so mad. *(Act out angry.)*

Then I think of Jesus, *(Fold hands.)*

And how much he loves me. *(Point to self.)*

I feel so very, very good *(Hug self.)*

And happy as can be. *(Raise arms, wave yellow streamer.)*

I think of all the many gifts *(Open arms wide.)*

That God has given me. *(Point to self.)*

I thank you, God, for feelings. *(Point to face.)*

I need them all you see. *(Hug self.)*

And I think of Jesus, *(Fold hands.)*

And how much he loves me. *(Point to self.)*

I feel so very, very good *(Hug self.)*

And happy as can be! *(Raise arms, wave yellow streamer.)*

Middle
Pass out a copy of *Activity Page 52* to each child. Read aloud the message on the top of the page. Remind the children that God always knows how we feel and that it is all right to have feelings. Explain that we have to learn what to do with our feelings. Encourage the children to suggest appropriate behavior when they are happy, sad or angry. Then have the children cut out the puppets and tape each one to a straw.

End
Help the children make a feelings graph. Cut three large circles from poster board and draw faces on them similar to those on *Activity Page 51.* Have the children select one of their streamers which shows how they are feeling today. Let them attach this streamer to the corresponding face.

Gather the children around the prayer table and lead them in the prayer found on the bottom of *Activity Page 52.*

Extra! Extra!

 Read the book *Mean Soup* by Betsy Everitt to the children.

All Stirred Up

Provide a cauldron or large pot and a spoon. Fill the cauldron or pot with red crepe paper streamers. Let the children yell into the cauldron or pot like in the story. Then give each child a turn to stir the cauldron or pot. Tell the children to stir away their anger. After all the children have had a turn to shout and stir, replace the red streamers in the cauldron or pot with yellow ones. Explain that we have gotten rid of our anger and now are filled with happy feelings.

Materials for Part 3:
- *Read to Me Page 53*
- yellow, blue, and red finger paint
- roll of white paper
- various kinds of music
- pans of yellow, blue, and red gelatin
- paper cups
- whipped topping
- spoons

I Have Feelings
(Part 3)

Theme: God always loves us.

Purpose:
• *to develop the awareness that God will love us no matter how we feel.*

Beginning

As the children enter the room, have Sudie Squirrel welcome them. Then help the children find the snowflakes with their names on them and place them on the tree.

Gather the children in a circle. Remind the children that we have been talking about our feelings. Tell the children that music affects our feelings. Play some music. Ask the children how they felt while listening. Try a different type of music, and repeat the question. Roll out a long sheet of white paper on the table. Have the children gather around the paper. Give each child three blobs of finger paint, one each of yellow, blue, and red. Play various kinds and tempos of music and encourage the children to finger paint to the music.

Middle

Pass out a copy of the *Read to Me Page 53* to each child. Call the children's attention to the illustrations. Ask them to find which children are happy, sad, or angry. Read the poem aloud to the children. Then ask the questions at the end. Encourage all the children to participate in the discussion.

End

Help the children prepare "A Feelings Snack." Ahead of time, prepare yellow, blue, and red gelatin in large shallow pans and allow to set. Cut these into cubes. Give each child a clear plastic cup. Have the children put several cubes of each of the three colors of gelatin in their cups. Tell the children that we are all made up of different feelings. All of our feelings together make us unique and special. Put a dollop of whipped topping on top of the gelatin cubes. Have the children use their fingers to draw a face in the topping that shows how they are feeling right now. Give the children spoons to enjoy their snacks. *Note: Be aware of any children with food allergies before using this activity.*

Gather the children around the prayer table and lead them in the following prayer: "Dear God, you understand my feelings. Help me to know what to do when I am feeling happy or sad or angry. Amen."

Extra! Extra!

 Read the story *Let's Paint a Rainbow* by Eric Carle.

Colorful Feelings

Experiment with color. Fill three clear plastic cups with water. In one cup, add yellow food coloring and stir to make yellow water. In another cup, add blue food coloring and stir to make blue water. In the third cup, add red food coloring and stir to make red water. Show these to the children and see whether they can remember what feelings are associated with each color (yellow—happy, blue—sad, and red—angry).

Pour a small amount of the yellow water into an empty cup. Add some red water. Ask the children what new color is made (*orange*). Ask the children to think of a different feeling that we could associate with orange. Suggest to the children that we could associate scary feelings with orange since that is a color we often see at Halloween.

Pour some of the yellow water in another empty cup. This time add some blue water. What color is made? (*green*) Ask the children to suggest another feeling to associate with this new color. Perhaps we could associate the feeling of excitement with the color green.

Finally, pour a small amount of red water in another empty cup. This time add some blue water. What color is made? (*purple*) Ask the children to think of another feeling that could be associated with the color purple. Suggest the feeling of confusion.

Review with the children that we all have many, many different feelings and that this is all right.

Materials for Lesson 14, Part 1:
- *Activity Page 55*
- popsicle sticks
- light blue construction paper
- brown craft foam
- shredded crinkled paper
- film container tops
- construction paper strips

Advent

Theme: During Advent we get ready for Christmas.

Purpose:
• *to affirm the children's experiences of waiting for Christmas by sharing the customs and traditions of the Advent season.*

Beginning

As the children enter the room, have Sudie Squirrel welcome them. Then help the children find the snowflakes with their names on them and place them on the tree.

Gather the children in a circle. Tell them that this is a special time of year. We call this time of year *Advent*. It lasts for about four weeks. It is the time we get ready to celebrate Christmas, the birthday of Jesus.

Ask the children to share stories of the ways their families get ready for Christmas. Do they decorate a tree? Shop for presents? Make surprises? Do they put up a nativity scene with Joseph, Mary, and their infant Jesus? Point out that although families may prepare for Christmas in different ways, we are all eagerly looking forward to celebrating Jesus' birthday.

Middle

Pass out a copy of *Activity Page 55* to each child. Draw the children's attention to the picture of an Advent wreath at the top of the page. Describe it to the children, explaining what it is made of. Point out that it has four candles to represent the four weeks of Advent. Ask them whether they have ever seen one at church or home.

Draw the children's attention to the picture puzzle. Tell them that inside this picture there are many hidden things that help us to know Christmas is coming. Ask the children to color the ones they find. Help as needed.

End

Help the children experience Advent by making an Advent countdown. Give each child a piece of light blue construction paper. Have the children glue two popsicle sticks in the shape of an "X" in the center of the page. Give the children a triangle cut from brown foam to attach to the top half of the "X" to make a manger. Give children shredded crinkle paper to glue into the manger for hay. Use the top of a film container as the head of baby Jesus and glue on top of the crinkle paper. Cut out a foam frame for each child and have him or her glue this around his or her picture.

Count how many days there are from today until Christmas with the children. Give each child this number of construction paper strips. Show the children how to make a paper chain with these strips. Attach this chain to the bottom of each child's picture. Tell the children that each day they are to tear off one ring from the chain. When the chain is all gone, it will be Christmas.

Gather the children around the prayer table and lead them in the following prayer: "Thank you, God, for the Advent season. It is such a joyful and exciting time for us to get ready to celebrate Jesus' birthday at Christmas. Amen."

Extra! Extra!

Read the book *Who Is Coming to Our House?* by Joseph Slate. Ask the children how the animals prepared for baby Jesus' visit.

Materials for Part 2:
- *Activity Page 56*
- 4 white candles
- pink and purple fabric paint
- small styrofoam or paper plates
- air-dry clay
- purple and pink birthday candles
- green paint

Advent
(Part 2)

Theme: We learn about the Advent wreath.

Purpose:
• *to enable the children to experience the custom of the Advent wreath.*

Beginning

As the children enter the room, have Sudie Squirrel welcome them. Then help the children find the snowflakes with their names on them and place them on the tree.

Gather the children in a circle or group. Show the children a picture of an Advent wreath. Explain that this is one tradition of the Advent season. Explain that we light one candle every day during the first week of Advent, two candles every day during the second week of Advent, three candles every day during the third week of Advent, and all four candles every day during the fourth week of Advent until Christmas day.

Tell the children that we will make an Advent wreath for our room. This wreath will be very special because each of them will help to make it. Tell the children that Advent wreaths have three purple candles and one pink candle. Show them four white pillar candles. Tell the children that we will use our thumbprints to make these candles the right colors. Help the children cover the candles with

thumbprints of fabric paint. Let these candles dry. The Advent wreath will be completed in Part 3 of this lesson.

Middle
Pass out a copy of *Activity Page 56* to each child. Tell the children that they will make an Advent wreath. Ask them to look at the illustrations. Remind the children that there are three purple candles and one pink candle on the Advent wreath, and the wreath itself should be green. Have the children cut out the candles and glue them where they belong.

End

Tell the children that we are going to make individual Advent wreaths to take home. Provide a small styrofoam or paper plate for each child. Give each child a small amount of air-dry clay. Show them how to roll the clay to form a "snake," then shape this "snake" into a circle. Have the children place the circle of clay on their plates. Insert three purple (or white with a purple ribbon tied around it if purple is unavailable) and one pink birthday candle into the clay. Allow to dry and harden. Remove the candles and help the children paint the clay green (markers can also be used to color the clay green). Replace the candles before sending home.

Conclude by leading the children in the prayer found at the bottom of *Activity Page 56*.

Extra! Extra!

Read the book *Jacob's Gift* by Max Lucado. Give each child an empty matchbox to use as a manger. Encourage the children to do kind things during Advent. Tell the children that each time they do something kind they should put a piece of straw or hay into the match box manger. Explain that the more nice things they do, the softer the bed will be for baby Jesus.

Materials for Part 3:
- *Read to Me Page 57*
- air-dry clay
- leaf-shaped cookie cutters
- green marker
- poster board

Advent
(Part 3)

Theme: We wait happily during Advent.

Purpose:
• *to help the children understand that during Advent we prepare to celebrate Jesus' birth.*

Beginning

As the children enter the room, have Sudie Squirrel welcome them. Then help the children find the snowflakes with their names on them and place them on the tree.

Gather the children around the table. Tell them that we will finish making the Advent wreath for our room. Give each child a small amount of air-dry clay. Have the children flatten this out and use leaf-shaped cookie cutters to make leaves for the wreath. (Children can also free-form leaves.) Have the children use green markers to color these. Cut a large circle from poster board. Cut out the center to form an "O." Place the four painted candles on this wreath. Have the children glue the leaves to the poster board to fill in between the candles.

Middle

Pass out a copy of *Read to Me Page 57* to each child. Call the children's attention to the illustrations around the page. Ask the children whether they can guess what the people are doing (*making an Advent wreath*). Then read the story to the children. Then ask the children the questions at the bottom of the page. Make sure the children realize that even though we wait to receive

personal gifts and joys at Christmas, the most important gift we are waiting for during Advent is the celebration of the birth of Jesus.

End

Gather the children in a circle on the floor. Teach the children the following song:

Christmas is Coming *(To the tune of "Did You Ever See a Lassie?")*

I know Christmas time is coming,
Is coming, is coming.
I know Christmas time is coming,
And I am so glad.

Put the wreath up on the doorway,
The doorway, the doorway.
Put the wreath up on the doorway
For Christmas is near.

Light the candles in the windows,
The windows, the windows.
Light the candles in the windows
For Christmas is near.

Gather the children around the prayer table. Bring the group Advent wreath made earlier. Lead the children in this blessing of the Advent Wreath.

Advent Wreath Blessing
This Advent Wreath, a circle of green
We place upon the table.
Each week a candle we shall light
Till Jesus' birth in the stable.
Oh, bless this wreath, dear God, we pray,
As we await your Son
To fill our lives with light and hope.
In him we shall be one.

100

Extra! Extra!

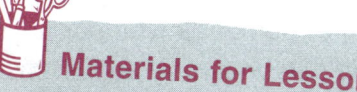 **An Advent Wreath Prayer Card**

Make a prayer card of prayers to say around the Advent wreath for the children to bring home. Copy the following prayer on a piece of tagboard for each child. Then have the children make a wreath around the prayer by dipping their thumbs in a green stamp pad and making thumbprints around the edge of the card. Painted toothpicks (pink and purple) can be attached to the card to resemble the candles on the Advent wreath.

Advent Wreath Prayer

We light the candles on this wreath
As we wait for Christmas Day,
When God gave Jesus, his own Son
To light our lives we pray.

Materials for Lesson 15, Part 1:
- *Activity Page 59*
- assortment of Christmas decorations
- white paint
- green construction paper
- glue
- glittery pipe cleaner
- hole punch, string or ribbon

Theme: Christmas is the day Jesus was born.

Purpose:
• *to focus the children's excitement on the traditions and family customs of Christmas.*

Beginning
Before the children arrive, put an assortment of Christmas decorations up around the room. As the children enter the room, have Sudie Squirrel welcome them. Then help the children find the snowflakes with their names on them and place them on the tree.

Gather the children in a circle and ask them whether they noticed anything different about the room. Encourage them to notice all the decorations around the room. Ask whether anyone knows why the room is decorated (*in celebration of Jesus' birthday, just as our homes are decorated when we have a birthday party*).

Tell the children that we are going to make some decorations to add to our room. We will make handprint angels to hang in our tree. Paint each child's hand with white paint and make two prints on green construction paper. Have the children keep fingers together with thumb extending out on one of the prints. When these handprints dry, cut them out. Overlap the handprints at an

angle, placing the palm of one hand over the palm of the other hand, and glue. Draw a face on the extended thumb and add a piece of glittery pipe cleaner for a halo. Punch a hole in the top, thread a piece of string or ribbon through the hole and tie in a knot. Hang these in the class tree.

Middle
Pass out a copy of *Activity Page 59* to each child. Call the children's attention to the Christmas star. Ask them why the star reminds them of Christmas. Invite the children to decorate and color their star however they would like. When they have finished, read aloud the paragraph at the top of the page. Encourage all the children to answer the questions.

End
Teach the children the following song:

 **Christmas** *(To the tune of "The Itsy, Bitsy Spider")*

**The little baby Jesus
Was born on Christmas Day.
Shepherds came along
And knelt down on the hay.**

**Dear Mother Mary
Held the babe that morn, and
We know the world was happy
To hear that Christ was born.**

Gather the children around the prayer table and lead them in the following prayer: "Dear God, thank you for giving us the gift of your Son, Jesus. Amen."

Extra! Extra!

Read one of these books to the children:
This Is the Star by Joyce Dunbar;
The Christmas Star by Marcus Pfister.

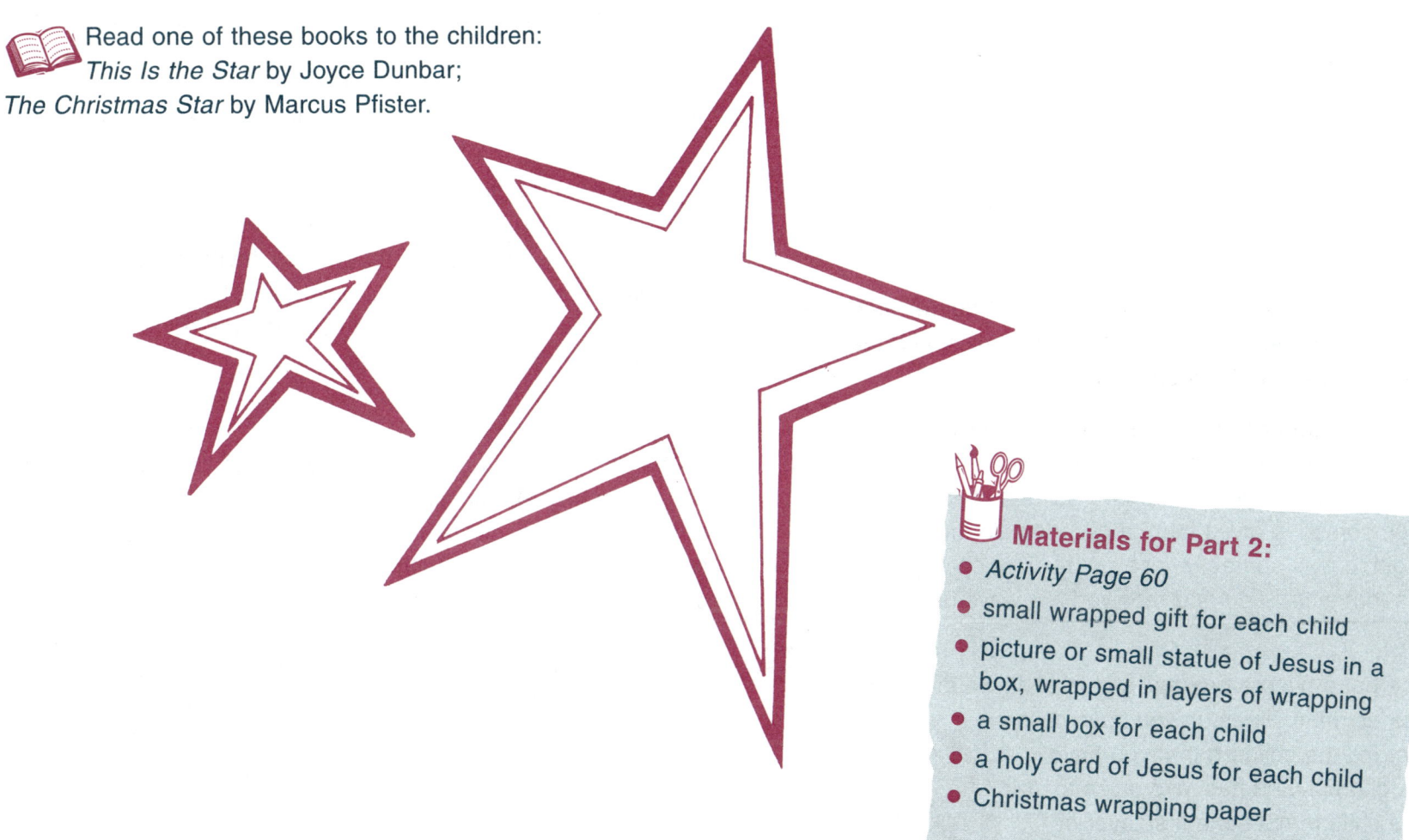

Materials for Part 2:
- *Activity Page 60*
- small wrapped gift for each child
- picture or small statue of Jesus in a box, wrapped in layers of wrapping
- a small box for each child
- a holy card of Jesus for each child
- Christmas wrapping paper

Christmas (Part 2)

Theme: Jesus is God's gift to us at Christmas.

Purpose:
• to present Jesus as the greatest of all God's gifts to us.

Beginning

As the children enter the room, have Sudie Squirrel welcome them. Then help the children find the snowflakes with their names on them and place them on the tree.

Gather the children around you and surprise them with a small wrapped gift for each of them to take home. Tell them that you gave them a gift because you love them. Ask the children how they feel when someone gives them a gift. How do they feel when they have a gift to give someone else? Why do people give us gifts? (Stress that gifts given and received are ways of showing love.)

Ahead of time put a picture or small statue of Jesus in a box. Wrap this box as many times as you have children in your group. Tell the children that you have given them a gift, but God has also given them a gift. Have one child remove the first layer of wrapping from the box. Then pass the gift to another child to remove the next layer of wrapping. Continue in this way until all the

children have had a turn removing a layer of wrapping, and the box is unwrapped. Open the box to reveal the statue or picture of Jesus. Explain to the children that God gives us Jesus, the greatest gift of all, at Christmas, and that Jesus is with us always.

Middle

Pass out a copy of *Activity Page 60* to each child. Read aloud the first paragraph at the top of the page. Ask the children how we thank God for the gift of Jesus. As the children respond, remind them that we can show God our thanks and love by what we say and do, and by the way we treat others. Invite the children to color the star and cut it out. Punch a hole in the top and thread a piece of string or ribbon through the hole. Encourage the children to take these home to hang on their trees.

End

Gather the children around you. Provide (or have the children bring from home) a small box for each child. Tell them that we will wrap a gift for our families. Explain that God gives us Jesus, the greatest gift of all, at Christmas. Then give each child a holy card with a picture of Jesus and have them place these in his or her box. Help the children wrap their boxes using Christmas wrapping paper. Tell the children to put these gifts under their trees at home. Encourage them to let their families open them on Christmas day. Have the children tell their families that these gifts remind us that God gives us Jesus on Christmas, and that Jesus is with us always.

Gather the children around the prayer table and lead them in the following prayer: "Dear God, thank you for giving us the gift of your Son, Jesus. Amen."

Extra! Extra!

Read the story *The Friendly Beasts, An Old English Christmas Carol* illustrated by Tomie dePaola. Teach the children the song that goes along with the story. Talk about the gifts that each animal gave to baby Jesus.

Materials for Part 3:
- *Read to Me Page 61*
- objects or pictures of items used to celebrate Christmas (Advent wreath, greeting cards, lights and candles, gifts)
- styrofoam cups
- wooden beads, styrofoam balls
- yarn or shredded crinkle paper
- sparkling pipe cleaner
- paper ribbon
- markers
- two wrapped boxes, two pictures or statues of Jesus
- round sugar cookies
- gel icing
- canned whipped cream
- sugar
- juice

Christmas (Part 3)

Theme: The story of Jesus' birth

Purpose:

• to present the story of the first Christmas.

Beginning

As the children enter the room, have Sudie Squirrel welcome them. Then help the children find the snowflakes with their names on them and place them on the tree.

Gather the children around you. Have a display of objects or pictures of items used to celebrate Christmas. Hold one up at a time as you explain each symbol and how it relates to Christmas. Some examples include:

• The *Advent wreath* reminds us to get ready for Christmas.

• *Greeting cards* are given to people to wish them peace and happiness at this holy season.

• *Lights and candles* remind us that Jesus is our light.

• *Gifts* are given to remind us that God gave us Jesus, the most precious gift of all.

Middle

Pass out a copy of *Read to Me Page 61* to each child. Tell the children that you are going to read the complete story of Christmas. Read aloud the story of Christmas, encouraging the children to look at the illustrations as you read. Then ask the questions at the bottom of the page. Encourage all the children to participate in the discussion.

End

Conclude the lesson with three centers. In the first center, help the children make a decoration for their tables at home. Give each child a styrofoam cup and have them place it upside down. Help the children glue a large wooden bead or a styrofoam ball on the top of the cup to make a head for the angel. Give the children yarn or shredded crinkled paper to attach for hair. Provide a piece of a sparkly pipe cleaner for a halo. Help the children attach a bow made from paper ribbon to the back of the cup to make the angel wings. Let the children add facial features with markers.

In the next center, have a "Gift Relay." Place two wrapped boxes under the tree in the class. Wrap the boxes so the lids may be taken off without unwrapping the gifts. Place a picture or statue of Jesus in each box. Set up two teams. Have the children on each team stand in two lines on the other side of the room from the tree. Have the first child on each team run to get the present under the tree and give it to the next child in line. This child opens the box, looks inside, and closes the box back up. He or she then runs back to the tree and places the gift back under the tree. Continue until all have had turns.

The last center is a snack center. Give each child a round sugar cookie. Provide gel icing to add facial features. Add two squirts of canned whipped cream on the plate to make wings. Invite the children to sprinkle the wings with sugar. Enjoy with juice. *Note: Be aware of any children with food allergies before using this activity.*

 Gather the children around the prayer table and sing the song "Christmas" found on page 102.

Extra! Extra!

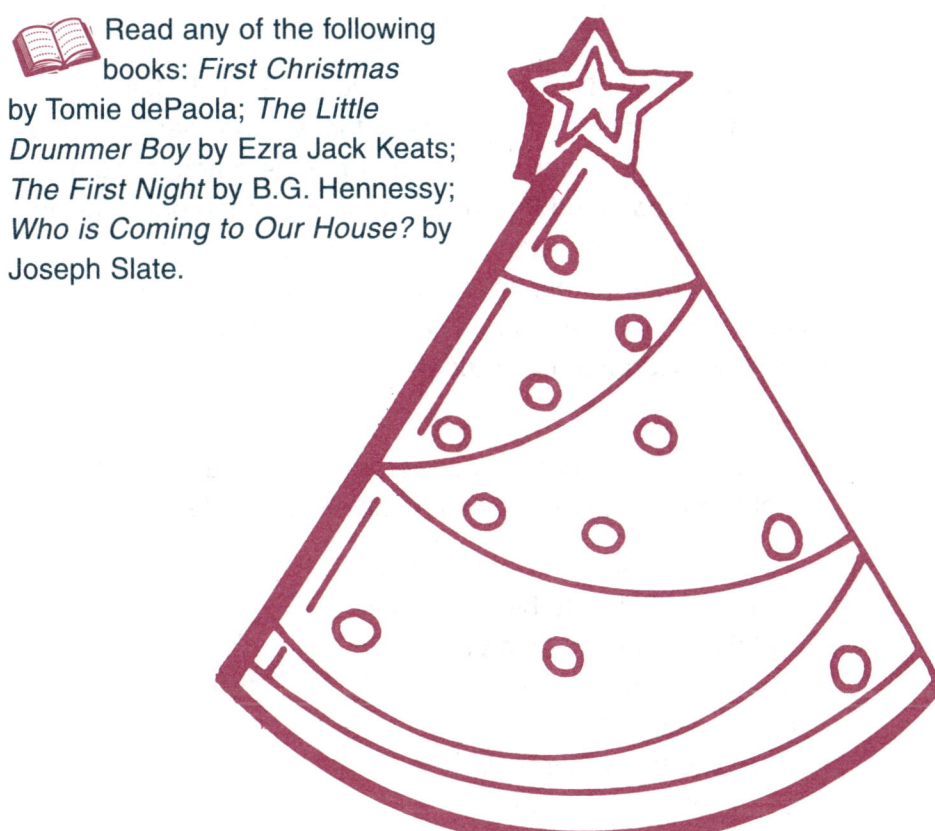 Read any of the following books: *First Christmas* by Tomie dePaola; *The Little Drummer Boy* by Ezra Jack Keats; *The First Night* by B.G. Hennessy; *Who is Coming to Our House?* by Joseph Slate.

 **Materials for Lesson 16, Part 1:**
- *Activity Page 63*
- children's Bible
- tagboard pictures, velcro, carpet square
- Sadlier's *Bible Felt Art Kit*
- white construction paper
- a seed for each child, glue

Theme: We know the Bible is a holy book.

Purpose:
• *to review the Bible stories of God's many gifts for us in creation.*

Beginning

As the children enter the room, have Sudie Squirrel welcome them. Then help the children find the snowflakes with their names on them and place them on the tree.

Gather the children around you. Recall with them the signs of God's love and goodness for all of God's creation: people, animals, fish, birds, land, sun, and water, and so on. Point out that creation is an ongoing expression of God's love and concern for us. People all over the world are dependent on God's gift of creation.

Remind the children that we learned about God's creation in the lesson about our wonderful world. Tell the children that Jesus used creation to tell stories about God our Father. We will hear one of these stories from the Bible now.

Read from a children's Bible or tell in your own words the first part of the story of the sower and the seed (Mark 4:1–10).

To enhance the experience, prepare pictures from the story on tagboard, color, and cut out. Attach a piece of sticky velcro to the back and put on a carpet square as you tell or read the story, or use Sadlier's *Bible Felt Art Kit.*

Middle
Pass out a copy of *Activity Page 63* to each child. Call the children's attention to the picture of the woman reading to the children. Ask the children whether someone reads to them from the Bible. Read aloud the words at the top of the page. Tell the children that on this page we read about God's creation. Have the children look at the happy faces of the children. Point out the picture of the land and sea. Then read the verse from Genesis. Invite the children to color the pictures.

End

Review the story of the sower and the seed. Have the children illustrate it in their Bible story booklets.

Ask the children what kind of soil they would like to be. Have them draw this kind of soil on a piece of white construction paper. Then give each child a seed to glue onto his or her "soil." Have the children use their crayons to draw what will grow from this seed.

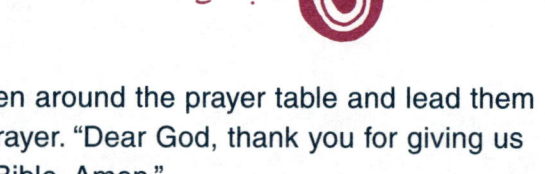

Gather the children around the prayer table and lead them in the following prayer. "Dear God, thank you for giving us your special book, the Bible. Amen."

Extra! Extra!

Soil and Seed Snack

Remind the children of the story of the sower and the seed. Then give each child a small zippered plastic bag with two chocolate sandwich cookies in it. Have the children crush these cookies, keeping the bag closed. Tell the children that they are "preparing the soil." Have the children pour the crushed cookies into a cup. Give each child a chocolate-covered raisin as a seed. Have the children poke a hole in the "soil" with their fingers and "plant" the seed. On the handle end of a plastic spoon, hot glue a flower cut from craft foam. Give one of these to each child to put in their "soil."

Materials for Part 2:
- *Activity Page 64*
- children's Bible
- tagboard pictures, velcro, carpet square
- popsicle sticks
- strips of brown construction paper
- glue or tape
- chocolate chip candy or candy wrapped as "coins"

109

More About the Bible (Part 2)

Theme: We listen to the Bible.

Purpose:
- *to help the children appreciate the word of God.*

Beginning

 As the children enter the room, have Sudie Squirrel welcome them. Then help the children find the snowflakes with their names on them and place them on the tree.

Gather the children in a circle around you. Tell the children that we will read another story from the Bible. Read from a children's Bible or tell in your own words the story of the woman and the lost coin (Luke 15:8–10). To enhance the experience, prepare pictures from the story on tagboard, color, and cut out. Attach a piece of sticky velcro to the back and put on a carpet square as you tell or read the story.

Have the children illustrate the story in their Bible booklets.

Middle

Pass out a copy of *Activity Page 64* to each child. Draw the children's attention to the picture at the bottom of the page. Explain that these are some of the many gifts that God created for us. Read the verse from Genesis at the bottom of the page. Have the children cut out the pictures and take these home to remember the story of creation.

End

 Have the children make a broom to help them remember the story they read from the Bible. Give each child a popsicle stick and a 2" by 8" strip of brown construction paper. Have the children cut slits in the brown construction paper, being careful not to cut all the way through. Then help the children roll this around the bottom of the popsicle stick to form a broom. Glue or tape in place. Give each child a chocolate chip, a doubloon, or a similar candy wrapped as a "coin." Encourage the children to take these home and use them as props when telling this story to their families.

Gather the children around the prayer table and lead them in the following prayer: "Dear God, help our hearts to always be open to your word. Amen."

Extra! Extra!

Find the Lost Coin

Cover a large cardboard circle with gold glitter. Hide this in the room, being careful not to make it too difficult to find. Have the children use their brooms to sweep the room until they find the coin. Give each child a turn to hide the coin.

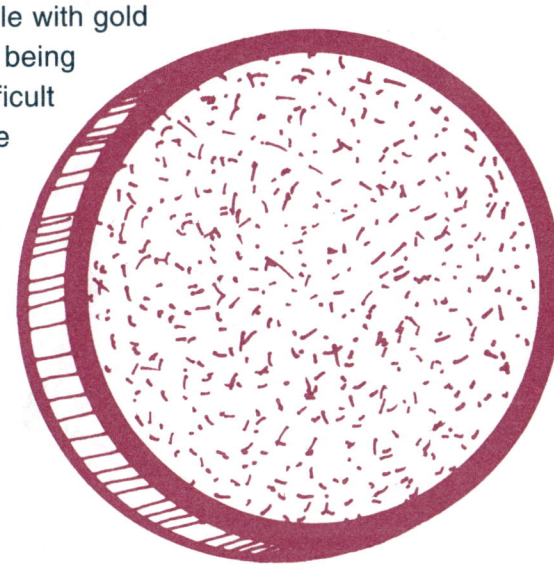

Materials for Part 3:
- props for Bible stories read or told in this lesson
- paper plates
- small round crackers
- cheese spread

More About the Bible
(Part 3)

Theme: In the Bible Jesus tells us how to love one another.

Purpose:

• *to help the children appreciate that in the Bible we have many wonderful stories of Jesus showing us how to love.*

Beginning

As the children enter the room, have Sudie Squirrel welcome them. Then help the children find the snowflakes with their names on them and place them on the tree.

Gather the children in a circle around you. Review the two Bible stories that were read in this lesson. Then have the children act each one out. Provide props as needed.

Middle

Provide a snack to remind the children of the story of the woman and the lost coin. Give each child a paper plate. On it place nine very small round crackers. Hide a tenth cracker under each child's napkin. Tell the children that they must find the tenth cracker before they can eat any. Once they find the "lost" cracker, invite children to put cheese spread on their crackers if desired. *Note: Be aware of any children with food allergies before using this activity.*

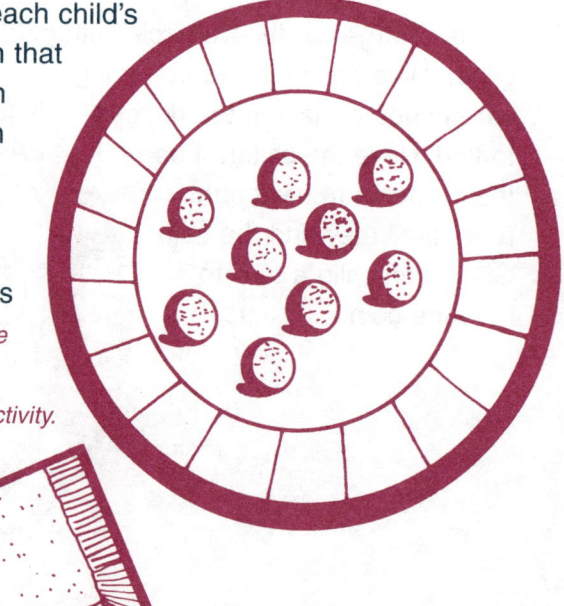

End

To conclude this unit, take down all the winter decorations around the room. Give the children the snowflakes with their names on them to take home. Explain to the children that when they come back to school, we will have something new with their names on them to hang on our tree.

Gather the children around the prayer table and lead them in the following prayer: "Dear God, thank you for giving us your special book, the Bible. Amen."

Extra! Extra!

A Special Bible Cloth

Remind the children that the Bible is a very special book. Tell the children that we will prepare a special cloth on which to keep this special book at home. Give each child a 10" by 12" piece of white fabric. Using white fabric paint, paint one entire finger of each child and have them print this on the cloth to make a candle. Then have the children dip their thumbs in yellow fabric paint and add a flame to the candle. Allow to dry thoroughly before sending home.

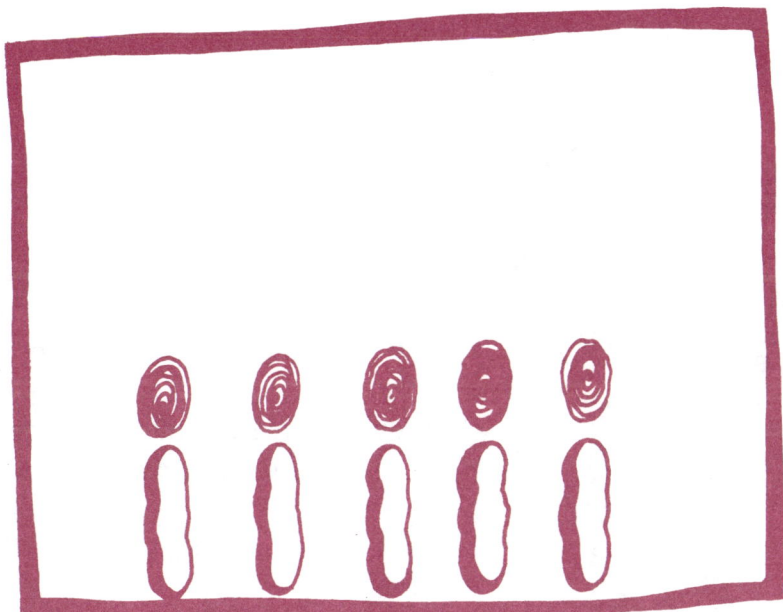

**Materials for Spring Unit Page:**

- *Spring Unit Page 65*
- spring items: bird's nest, seeds, flowers, eggs, pictures of baby animals, an umbrella, shamrocks, tennis shoes and so on
- empty paper towel spools
- brown paint
- glue
- green and pink tissue paper squares
- rice cakes
- popsicle sticks or plastic knives
- softened cream cheese
- strawberry jam
- rectangular wheat crackers

Unit 3
Belonging to My Family

Theme: Celebrating Spring

Beginning

A small tree should be attached to the wall at the children's eye level. Prepare a flower from construction paper for each child with his or her name on it. As each child enters the preschool room, he or she should find the flower with his or her name on it and attach it to the tree.

Introduce the season of spring by bringing in items that are particular to this time of year. Some items might include a bird's nest, seeds, flowers, eggs, pictures of baby animals, an umbrella, shamrocks, tennis shoes, and so on. Gather the children and show them these objects. Talk about the season of spring. Explain that in spring, the weather starts to get a little warmer and the trees begin to grow once again. The trees begin to bud. These buds blossom into flowers.

Teach the children the following song:

♫ **Spring Is Here** *(To the tune of "Frère Jacques")*

Spring is here, spring is here.
Warmer days, warmer days,
Tulips, eggs, and bunnies; tulips, eggs, and bunnies;
Celebrate! Celebrate!

Middle

Pass out a copy of the *Unit Page* to each child. Explain that the pictures show people having fun doing things in spring. Invite the children to make up a story about each picture. Ask the children what they like to do in spring.

End

Make a spring tree. Give each child an empty paper towel spool. Have the children paint this brown. Cut several slits in the top and bend the strips outward to form branches. Have the children put a thin layer of glue on these branches. Give the children green and pink tissue paper squares. Show them how to crumple the squares and stick them onto the glue-covered branches.

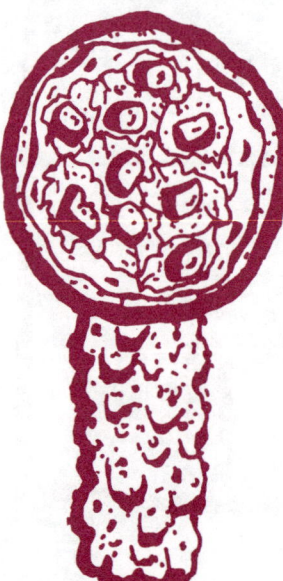

For a snack, make "Special Spring Trees" together. Give each child a large round corn chip. Have the children use popsicle sticks or plastic knives to spread sour cream, plain yogurt, or softened cream cheese on the chip. Sprinkle on shredded lettuce and chopped tomatoes to give the appearance of blossoms on the tree. Give each child a fat pretzel stick to use as a tree trunk. Enjoy with fruit juice. *Note: Be aware of any children with food allergies before using this activity.*

Extra! Extra!

 A Handprint Spring Tree

Paint each child's forearm brown (the tree-trunk) and stamp this onto a piece of light blue construction paper. Paint the child's hand (with fingers open wide) green and pink. Help the child stamp this at the top of the trunk to complete the tree.

 Read any of the following books:

My Spring Robin by Anne Rockwell, published by Simon & Schuster's Children's Books, (New York) 1996.

When Will It Be Spring? by Catherine Walters, published by NAL/Dutton, (New York) 1998.

Clifford's Spring Clean-Up by Norman Bridwell, published by Scholastic, Inc., (New York) 1997.

Hopper Hunts for Spring by Marcus Pfister, published by North-South Books, (New York) 1995.

April Showers by George Shanon, published by William Morrow & Company, (New York) 1995.

Additional Suggestions for Storytime During Unit 3

Bridwell, Norman. *Clifford's Family.* New York: Scholastic, Inc., 1990.

_____. *Clifford's Happy Easter.* New York: Scholastic, Inc., 1994.

Brown, Margaret Wise. *The Runaway Bunny.* New York: HarperCollins Children's Books, 1997.

Carle, Eric. *A House for Hermit Crab.* New York: Simon & Schuster, 1990.

_____. *The Very Lonely Firefly.* New York: The Putnam Publishing Group, 1994.

Cohen, Miriam. *Bee My Valentine.* New York: Bantam Doubleday Dell Books for Young Readers, 1995.

Damon, Laura. *Secret Valentine.* Mahwah, NJ: Troll Communications L.I.C., 1991.

Freeman, Don. *Corduroy's Easter.* New York: Penguin Putnam, 1999.

Joosse, Barbara M. *I Love You the Purplest.* San Francisco, CA: Chronicle Books, 1996.

_____. *Mama, Do You Love Me?* San Francisco, CA: Chronicle Books, 1998.

King, Stephen Michael. *A Special Kind of Love.* New York: Scholastic, Inc., 1996.

McBrateny, Sam. *Guess How Much I Love You.* Cambridge MA: Candlewick Press, 1995.

Pfister, Marcus. *Rainbow Fish to the Rescue.* New York: North-South Books, 1995.

Materials for Lesson 17, Part 1:
- *Activity Page 67*
- various representations of families
- construction paper hearts

Theme: Our families love and care for us.

Purpose:

• *to help the children deepen their awareness that God's gifts of life and love come to us through our families.*

Beginning

As the children enter the room, have Sudie Squirrel welcome them. Then help the children find the flowers with their names on them and place them on the tree.

Gather the children in a circle. Focus on families by showing representations of families to the group, such as photographs of your own family, paper dolls, colorform or flannel board families. Explain that these are all families because they belong to one another. Point out that there are many different types of families. Some are big and some are small, but all families love and care for one another.

Middle

Pass out a copy of *Activity Page 67* to each child. Call the children's attention to the pictures of human and animal parents. Encourage the children to name each set of parents. Then tell the children that on the right side of the paper are the babies of these parents. Ask the children whether they can figure out which baby belongs with each set of parents. Read aloud the paragraphs at the top of the page. Then have the children cut out the pictures of the babies and paste them with their parents.

End

Give each child a heart cut from construction paper. Go around to each child and help him or her cut that heart into the same number of pieces as the number of people in that child's family. Have the children draw a face of one family member in each piece. Help the children put the pieces together to complete their hearts. Explain that families are made up of many people who love and care for each other.

Gather the children around the prayer table and lead them in the following prayer: "Dear God, thank you for giving us our families. Amen."

Extra! Extra!

Read the book *Clifford's Family* by Norman Bridwell.

God Gave Me My Family
(To the tune of "London Bridge")

God gave me my family
Family, family.
God gave me my family
To love and care for me.
My family loves and cares for me,
Cares for me, cares for me.
My family loves and cares for me,
And I say, "Thank you, God!"

**Materials for Part 2:**
- *Activity Page 68*
- a scrapbook of family activities
- magazine pictures of families
- construction paper

Belonging to My Family (Part 2)

Theme: Families have wonderful stories to tell.

Purpose:

• *to help the children appreciate that families have wonderful stories to tell.*

Beginning

As the children enter the room, take a picture of each one using an instant camera. Then have Sudie Squirrel welcome them. Help the children find the flowers with their names on them and place them on the tree.

Gather the children in a circle. Tell the children that we have been talking and learning about families. Point out that although no two families are exactly alike, all families are equally important to the people within them. Each family has their own set of customs, traditions, and ways of doing things. Encourage the children to discuss some of the special things they do as a family. If possible, bring in a scrapbook or pictures of activities with your own family to share with the children. Ask the children whether their families have scrapbooks. Stress that God loves all families.

Middle

Pass out a copy of *Activity Page 68* to each child. Remind the children that each family has its own stories about family members and about things that have happened in the family. These stories tend to be told in the family again and again through the years.

Share some of your own favorite family stories with the group. Invite the children to tell their own stories. Then encourage the children to draw or color their story in the empty space on *Activity Page 68*.

End

Show the children pictures cut from magazines of families doing things together. Ask the children to find a picture of something their family does together either already cut out or in a magazine. Have the children cut this picture out and mount it on a piece of construction paper. Have the child tell you what his or her family does that is like the picture and write it on the paper. Save this page for the children's scrapbooks.

My family likes to go bowling.

Gather the children around the prayer table. Lead them in saying the prayer found at the bottom of *Activity Page 68*.

Extra! Extra!

Read the book A *Special Kind of Love* by Stephen Michael King. Give each child a box. Have the children recall all the things the dad in the story made for his son from boxes. Then have the children work together to make something special from their boxes.

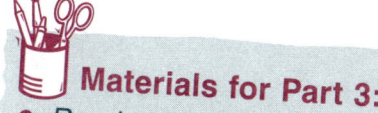

Materials for Part 3:
- *Read to Me Page 69*
- tagboard
- stamps and stickers

119

Belonging to My Family (Part 3)

Theme: The Holy Family is our model.

Purpose:
• *to introduce to the children the story of the Holy Family.*

Beginning

As the children enter the room, have Sudie Squirrel welcome them. Then help the children find the flowers with their names on them and place them on the tree.

Gather the children in a circle on the floor. Remind the children that God gave us Jesus to show us how to live a good and happy life. Tell them that Jesus grew up in a family who loved and cared for him just as families love and care for children today, all over the world.

Teach the children the following song:

♫ The Holy Family *(To the tune of "Old MacDonald")*

Jesus had a family
Just like you and me.
His family loved him oh so much,
Just like mine loves me.

With a clap, clap, here,
And a clap, clap, there,
Here a clap,
There a clap,
Everywhere a clap, clap.
Jesus had a family
Just like you and me.

Middle

Pass out a copy of *Read to Me Page 69* to each child. Draw the children's attention to the picture of the Holy Family. Tell the children that you are going to read a story about Jesus' family. Read the story aloud. Ask the questions at the end of the story. Encourage all the children to participate in the discussion.

End

Make a prayer card with a prayer to the Holy Family. Copy the following prayer on a piece of tagboard for each child. Invite the children to decorate their prayer cards with stamps or stickers. Encourage the children to bring these home and say this prayer with their families.

Prayer to the Holy Family
Jesus, Mary, and Joseph, too,
I pray to you this day.
Bless my family, keep them safe
In each and every way.

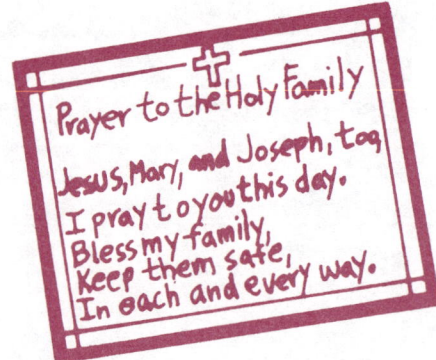

Gather the children around the prayer table with their prayer cards. Lead them in the prayer found on their prayer cards.

Extra! Extra!

Jesus in the Temple

Read from a children's Bible or tell in your own words the story of Jesus in the temple (Luke 2:41–52). Explain to the children that this is a story about Jesus when he was a child. After reading the story, have the children act it out. Then have the children illustrate it in their Bible story booklets.

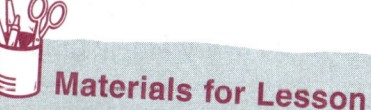

Materials for Lesson 18, Part 1:
- *Activity Page 71*
- pictures of various families
- white construction paper
- popsicle sticks (five for each child)
- sponges
- markers

All Kinds of Families

Theme: There are many different kinds of families.

Purpose:

• *to help the children appreciate that there are many different kinds of families.*

Beginning

As the children enter the room, have Sudie Squirrel welcome them. Then help the children find the flowers with their names on them and place them on the tree.

Gather the children in a circle on the floor. Remind them that God gave us families to love and care for us. Point out that a family usually is two parents and several children. Or a family may be one parent and several children. Or a family may be just one parent and one child. God loves every family group no matter how large or small.

Show the children pictures of families (two-parent families, one-parent families, one child, few children, many children). As you present each picture, talk about the family members. Then go around the circle and ask the children who belongs to their family group. Be sure to stress again at the end of the discussion that God loves all families, large or small. God made all people and families different, but he loves and cares for us all the same.

Middle

Pass out a copy of *Activity Page 71* to each child. Read aloud the message at the top of the page. Remind the children that all families, big or small, belong to God. Let the children do the activity by drawing or coloring in each member of their families. Explain that a house or an apartment is only a building; it's the warmth and security of the family members that make it a home.

End

Make a group book of special families. Give each child a piece of white construction paper and five popsicle sticks. Help the children glue the sticks into the shape of a house on the paper. Give the children a sponge cut in the shape of a circle and have them sponge-paint one circle inside the house for each member in their families. When the paint is dry, encourage the children to add facial features and hair to the circles using markers. Write the family name across the bottom of the page. Bind all the children's pages together to create a book of special families. Leave this book out for the children to enjoy.

Bring the book of special families to the prayer table and lead the children in the following prayer: "Thank you, God, for the people in our families. Amen."

Extra! Extra!

 A Family Graph

On a large piece of bulletin board or freezer paper, make a row for each child and place their family name at the left. Dip people-shaped sponges or people-shaped cookie cutters into paint and have the children print their family members in their rows.

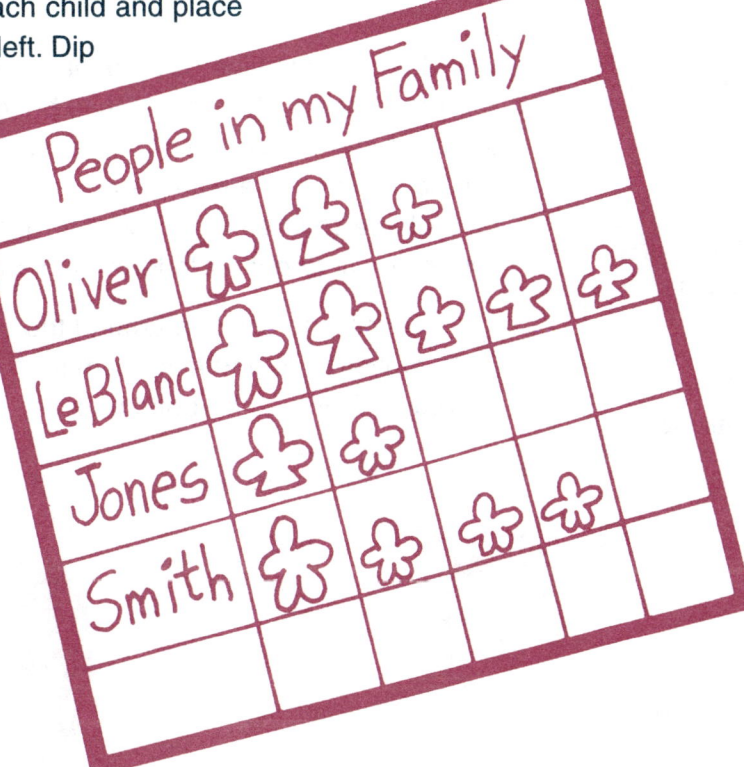

Materials for Part 2:
- *Activity Page 72*
- index cards or white construction paper
- purple stamp pad or paint
- green marker
- paper twist ribbon

123

All Kinds of Families (Part 2)

Theme: God loves and cares for us through our families.

Purpose:

• *to help the children appreciate the mutual love and caring in their families.*

Beginning

As the children enter the room, have Sudie Squirrel welcome them. Then help the children find the flowers with their names on them and place them on the tree.

Gather the children around the table. Tell the children that our families are made up of individuals. Give each child a small index card or piece of white construction paper. Have the children put one purple thumbprint for each member of their families on this card, putting the prints close together to form a bunch of grapes. Have the children use a green marker to add a stem. Keep these for an activity at the end of this lesson.

Middle

Pass out a copy of *Activity Page 72* to each child. Read aloud the message on the top of the page. Ask the children to recall how they help in their families. Ask them how others in the family help them. Have the children draw or color a picture of their family helping and caring for one another. Help the children as needed.

End

Make a large vine using paper twist ribbon. Place this at the prayer table. Have each child bring his or her bunch of grapes prepared in the first part of this lesson. Call each child by name and have the child attach his or her bunch of grapes to the vine. After all the children have had a turn, explain that all of our families come together to form the family of God.

Gather the children around the prayer table and lead them in the prayer found at the bottom of *Activity Page 72.*

Extra! Extra!

 Read the book *I Love You the Purplest* by Barbara M. Joosse.

 A New Bunch

Give each child a small amount of red clay and a small amount of blue clay. Explain that both these colors are pretty by themselves, but when we mix them together, they form a new color that is also very pretty. Have the children mix the two colors of clay together, kneading them until purple is produced. Then have them break off small pieces of purple clay and roll these into balls. Show the children how to glue these balls together on a plate to make a bunch of grapes.

Tell the children that each member in a family is special by themselves, just like the colors of red and blue. But when a family works together, something new and wonderful—like the color purple—is formed.

Materials for Part 3:
- *Read to Me Page 73*
- pictures of homes in various styles
- lunch-size brown paper bags
- newspaper
- lunch-size white paper bags

All Kinds of Families
(Part 3)

Theme: We belong to our families.

Purpose:
• *to help the children appreciate that all families are special and loved by God.*

Beginning

As the children enter the room, have Sudie Squirrel welcome them. Then help the children find the flowers with their names on them and place them on the tree.

Gather the children in a circle around you. Show the children a variety of pictures of different styles of homes. Be sure to include apartments, condos, and mobile homes, as well as houses. Let the children talk about where they live. Stress that it doesn't matter whether a home is big or small, plain or fancy, or how many times families may have moved; what is important is that the families who live within the homes are loved and needed.

Teach the children the following fingerplay:

Helping

Five little children (*Hold up hand with five fingers.*)
In a family,
Working, playing, singing, (*Shake hands about.*)
Happy as can be.

This one is helping (*Raise thumb.*)
Mother (Father) care for me.
This one is sharing (*Raise pointer.*)
And taking turns you see.

This one is talking (*Raise middle finger.*)
In a loving way.
This one is helping (*Raise ring finger.*)
Put the toys away.

This last one is happy (*Raise pinky.*)
It's so much fun to share.
Children in a family (*Clasp hands together.*)
Show us all they care.

Middle

Pass out a copy of *Read to Me Page 73* to each child. Have the children look at the illustrations as you read the story. Ask the children to share their feelings about this story. Encourage all the children to participate in the discussion.

End

Help the children make paper bag homes. Give each child a lunch-size brown paper bag and have him or her stuff this with newspaper. Then help the children slip a white bag, the same size, over the stuffed bag, so the white bag is upside down. Give the children markers and have them draw windows and doors on the white bag. Give each child another brown lunch bag, keeping it folded flat. Tell the children to cut the bottom of the bag off while the bag is still flat. Open up the bottom to form a triangular shape. Attach this to the top of the white bag to form a roof. Have the children use markers to add shingles.

Gather the children around the prayer table and lead them in the following prayer: "Dear God, thank you for the gift of our families. Amen."

126

Extra! Extra!

 Read the book *A House for Hermit Crab* by Eric Carle.

A House for Hermit Crab

Give each child a pointed sugar ice cream cone. Have the children cover the cone with white icing. Encourage the children to decorate the "house" with candy sprinkles, chocolate chips, candy-coated chocolates, red cinnamon candies, and so on. Give each child a vanilla wafer to make a crab. Add eyes using materials available. Using small dabs of icing, attach broken pretzels or pieces of licorice whip for the legs. Set the crab in his "house."

 **Materials for Lesson 19, Part 1:**
- *Activity Page 75*
- craft foam
- fabric paint
- magnet strips

19 Showing Love

Theme: We learn to love in our families.

Purpose:

• *to affirm the ways we show love in our families.*

Beginning

 As the children enter the room, have Sudie Squirrel welcome them. Then help the children find the flowers with their names on them and place them on the tree.

Gather the children in a circle on the floor. Tell the children that there are many things families and relatives do for them in their homes that show their families' love for them. Have Sudie Squirrel share some of the things her family does for her, such as: her mom feeds her nuts, her dad reads her a bedtime story, and her brother plays games with her. Invite the children to share similar situations from their families.

Teach the children the following song:

♫ Showing Love *(To the tune of "Old MacDonald")*

God gave me a family.
God is good to me.
We work and share,
And laugh and play,
In my family!

With a big hug here,
And a big hug there,
Here a hug,
There a hug,
Everywhere a hug, hug.
God gave me a family.
God is good to me.

Middle

Pass out a copy of *Activity Page 75* to each child. Call the children's attention to the pictures in the hearts. Ask them what they think is happening in each picture. Who are the people? Why is the child hugging the man?

Remind the children that hugging shows we love someone. Ask the children to draw or color a picture of themselves showing love to someone else. Read the verse from the Gospel of John to the children. Why is it in a heart?

End

Help the children to make a frame for a family picture. Cut a rectangle from craft foam. Cut out the center of the rectangle, leaving a one- to two-inch wide frame. Show children how to make thumbprint hearts around the frame using fabric paint. Attach a strip of magnet to the back. Encourage the children to bring these home, put a picture of their families in them, and hang them on their refrigerators.

Gather the children around the prayer table and lead them in the following prayer: "Dear God, thank you for giving me a family. Amen."

Extra! Extra!

Read the book *Guess How Much I Love You* by Sam McBrateny.

This Much!

After sharing this story with the children, have them cut a heart from red construction paper. Write the words *I Love You This Much* across the heart. Then have each child stand with arms spread open wide. Cut a piece of adding machine tape the size of the child's armspread. Attach this to the child's heart. Encourage the children to bring these home to their mothers.

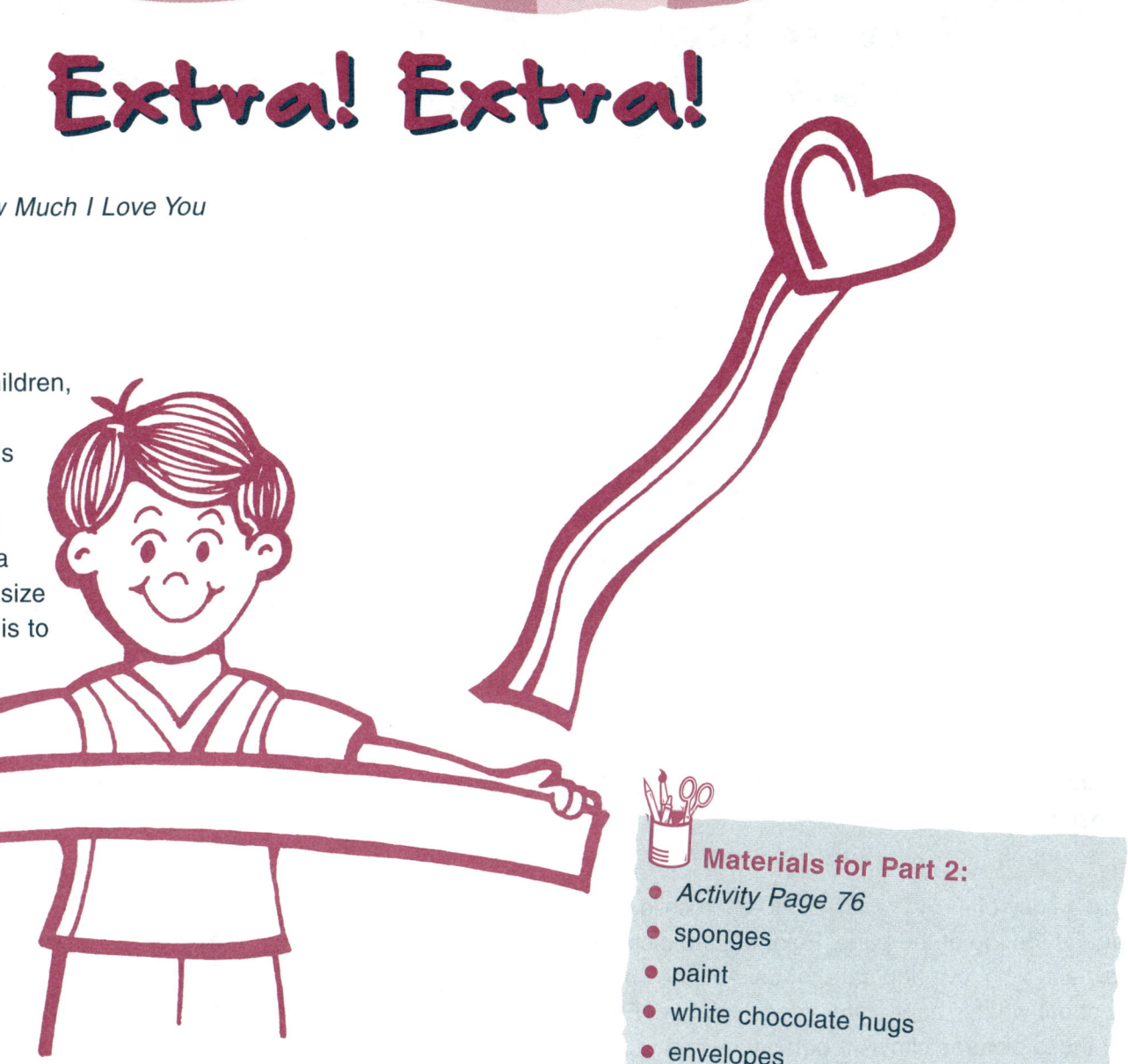

Materials for Part 2:
- *Activity Page 76*
- sponges
- paint
- white chocolate hugs
- envelopes

Showing Love
(Part 2)

Theme: We are learning to recognize who loves us.

Purpose:
• *to help the children recognize good touches from people who care for us, who love us, and whom we can trust.*

Beginning

As the children enter the room, have Sudie Squirrel welcome them. Then help the children find the flowers with their names on them and place them on the tree.

Gather the children in a circle or group. Let Sudie Squirrel go around the circle and give each child a hug. Remind the children that a hug shows love. Then invite each child to come up one at a time and tell whether he or she has ever been hugged. Encourage the child to share who has hugged him or her. Ask the child why this person hugged him or her. Be sure to give each child a turn to share experiences.

Middle

Pass out a copy of *Activity Page 76* to each child. Read aloud the message at the top of the page. Point out the pictures of the people we know and who love and care for us. Ask the children to make up a story about what is happening in each picture. Emphasize that each of these pictures shows a person we can trust.

Invite the children to act out each of the stories told. Then have the children cut out the hearts and punch holes in the tops.

Thread yarn or string through the holes and tie in a knot. Have the children hang these on the tree with their names on them or on a Friendship Tree in the kindergarten room.

End

Gather the children around the table. Have Sudie go around the group and give each child a white chocolate hug. Then tell the children we will share one of these with a member of our families. Give each child an envelope with the following poem written on it:

I have a little hug,
A gift for you today,
To tell you that I love you
In each and every way.

Have the children sponge paint hearts on the envelope. When they are dry, have the children put one white chocolate hug in the envelope and seal it. Encourage the children to bring this home and give it to someone in their family that they would like to show love to.

Gather the children around the prayer table and lead them in the following prayer: "Thank you, God, for all the members of my family. Help me always show that I love them. Amen."

Extra! Extra!

Read the book *The Runaway Bunny* by Margaret Wise Brown. Explain to the children that Mother Bunny showed love to her child by always following him wherever he went. She gave her child carrots to eat because that was his favorite food. Share some carrot sticks with the children.

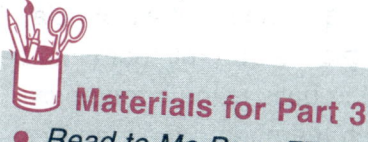

Materials for Part 3:
- *Read to Me Page 77*
- air-dry clay
- toothpicks
- markers
- yarn

Showing Love
(Part 3)

Theme: We learn to recognize good touches as signs of love.

Purpose:

• *to help the children understand "good touches" and that not all touching is good touching.*

Beginning

As the children enter the room, have Sudie Squirrel welcome them. Then help the children find the flowers with their names on them and place them on the tree.

Gather the children in a circle or group. Sing the song "Showing Love," found on page 128, with the children.

Then tell the children that we will make "Family Necklaces." Give each child a small amount of air-dry clay. Have the children break off small pieces and roll them into balls. Have the children make holes in the balls using a toothpick. Tell the children to make one ball for each member in their families, including themselves. Then have the children draw their family members' faces on each of the balls of clay, using markers. Allow to dry.

Middle

Pass out a copy of *Read to Me Page 77* to each child. Call the children's attention to the illustrations. Ask them whether they have ever been to a zoo. Have they seen baby animals with their mothers? Explain that this is a story about a mother monkey and her little baby monkey. Read the story aloud. Discuss as appropriate for your group.

End

Gather the children around you at a table. Give each child a toothpick with a long piece of yarn or string taped to it. Have the children use this as a "needle and thread" to string the beads made in the beginning of this lesson. When all the beads are on the yarn or string, cut off the toothpick and tie the ends into a knot. Let the children wear their family necklaces.

Gather the children around the prayer table and lead them in the following prayer: "Dear God, help me to always know when good people love me and to love them, too. Amen."

Extra! Extra!

 Read the book *Mama, Do You Love Me?*
by Barbara M. Joosse.

 **Materials for Lesson 20, Part 1:**
- *Activity Page 79*
- pictures of earlier kindergarten celebrations
- white construction paper
- sponges
- paint

20 Celebrating with My Family

Theme: Celebrations are fun.

Purpose:

• *to help the children to be part of a celebrating community.*

Beginning

As the children enter the room, have Sudie Squirrel welcome them. Then help the children find the flowers with their names on them and place them on the tree.

Gather the children in a circle or group. Tell the children we have special holidays each year to celebrate with our families: Halloween, Thanksgiving, Christmas, Valentine's Day, Easter, and our own individual birthdays. If possible, show pictures taken from kindergarten celebrations. Invite the children to tell about special things their families do on the holidays. Explain that, just as we have many holidays, we have many ways to celebrate them. Each family does things in its own special way, and that's fine. Teach the following song:

♫ **My Family** *(To the tune of "Pop Goes the Weasel")*

Happy, happy, happy am I,
For God gave me a family.
We work, we play, and we share a lot.
Hooray for my family!

Our days are very busy,
We all have lots to do.
But we still love and care a lot.
Hooray for my family!

(Repeat verse1.)

Our days are filled with work
and with play.
We all have fun together.
Then we pray our thanks to
God.
Hooray for my family!

Middle

Pass out a copy of *Activity Page 79* to each child. Read aloud the message and the instructions at the top of the page. Then draw the children's attention to the four items pictured at the bottom of the page. Have the children name the items. Then talk about where each item may fit on the table. Have the children cut out each item and paste it on the table. Help as needed. In the white space at the bottom right, ask the children to draw something they could add to the table to set it for one of the holidays.

End

Help the children make a placemat for a special celebration. Give each child a large piece of white construction paper. Show the children how to cut off the corners to make an oval. Write on each child's placemat the words *You Are Special*. Then have the children decorate their placemats by sponging various colors of hearts. Allow to dry. Laminate if possible. Encourage the children to take these home and use them whenever there is a special celebration at home.

Gather the children around the prayer table and lead them in the following prayer: "Thank you, God, for celebrations! Amen."

Extra! Extra!

The Year-End Scrapbook

Make a page to add to the children's scrapbooks. Give each child a piece of paper. Have the children illustrate a favorite family celebration. Go around and write on each child's page what celebration is illustrated, what foods are eaten at this celebration, who comes to this celebration, and why the child loves this celebration so much. Add these pages to the children's scrapbooks.

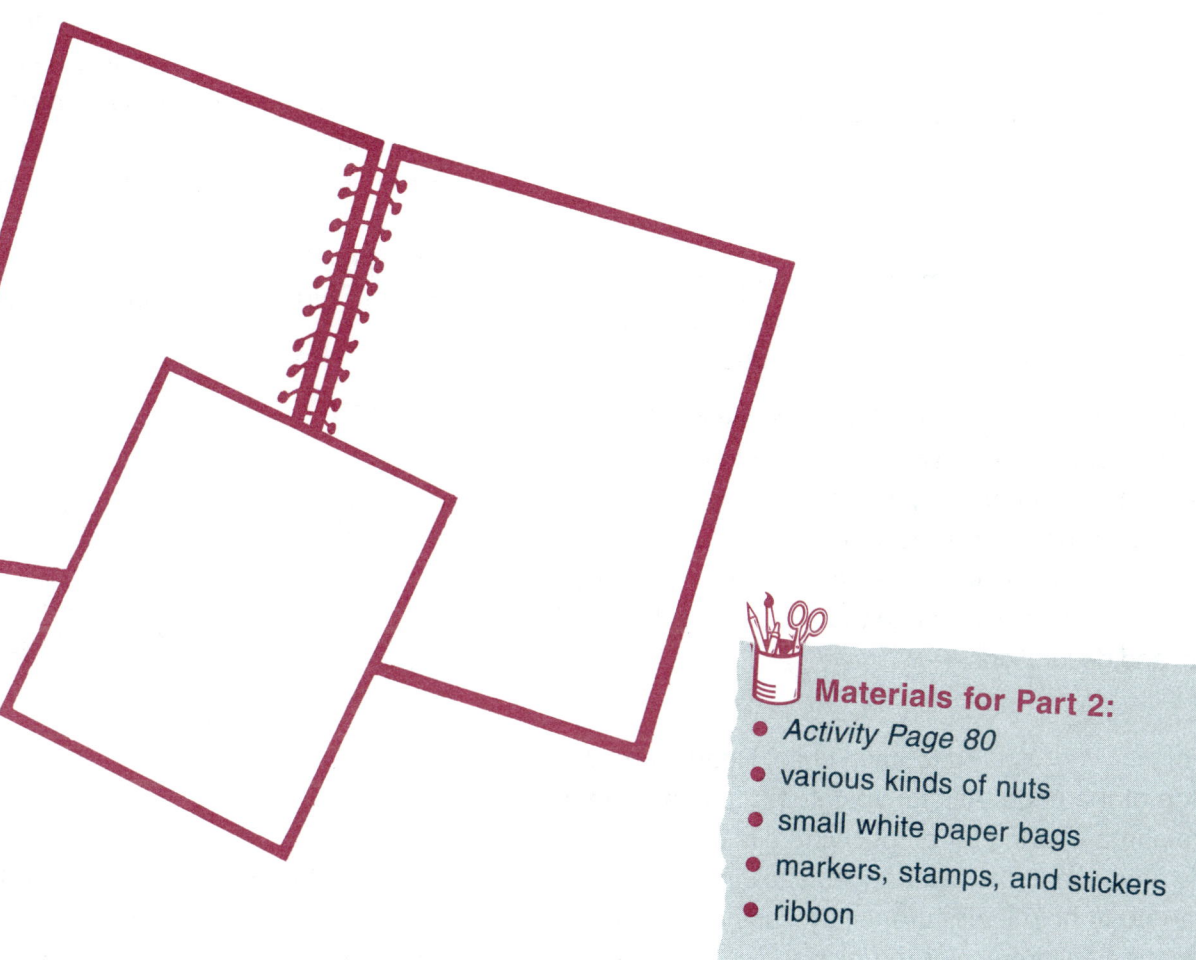

Materials for Part 2:
- *Activity Page 80*
- various kinds of nuts
- small white paper bags
- markers, stamps, and stickers
- ribbon

Celebrating with My Family (Part 2)

Theme: We can help in family celebrations.

Purpose:
• *to help the children experience taking part in preparing for and enjoying family celebrations.*

Beginning

As the children enter the room, have Sudie Squirrel welcome them. Then help the children find the flowers with their names on them and place them on the tree.

Gather the children in a circle on the floor. Tell them that it will soon be Sudie Squirrel's birthday. The next time they come to kindergarten, we will help Sudie celebrate her birthday. Explain that we will all have to work together now to make this a special celebration because we are Sudie's kindergarten family. Ask the children to name some things we will need for the celebration. Encourage them to include things such as food, gifts, and decorations.

Middle

Pass out a copy of *Activity Page 80* to each child. Read aloud the message at the top of the page. Ask for volunteers to share other ways they may help in preparing for a special family celebration. Call the children's attention to the illustrations showing some things children can do to help their parents. Discuss the pictures one at a time. Have the children color the pictures of the things they can do to help their families.

End

Ahead of time, scatter various kinds of nuts around the playground or in another room. Then tell the children that we are going to prepare a gift for Sudie. Remind the children that Sudie's favorite food is nuts. Explain that we will gather nuts for Sudie's gift. Give each child a small white paper bag. Have the children use markers, stamps, and stickers to decorate their bags. Then take the children outside or into the other room. Have the children gather nuts and put them in their bags. After all the nuts have been picked up, bring the children back into the room. Use a piece of ribbon and tie the bags closed. Tell the children that we cannot tell Sudie what is in her gifts. Keep these at school for Sudie's birthday party in Part 3 of this lesson.

Gather the children around the prayer table. Lead them in the following prayer: "Dear God, thank you for celebrations and families. May we always help our families as they prepare for celebrations. Amen."

Extra! Extra!

🔵 Happy Birthday, Sudie Squirrel!

Help the children make a tablecloth for Sudie's birthday celebration. Use a purchased paper tablecloth or a large piece of bulletin board paper. Show the children how to make handprint acorns on the tablecloth using their handprints. Paint the children's hands with light brown paint. Have them make prints along the edge of the tablecloth by pressing their hands on the paper with fingers together and pointing down. Paint the children's hands again, this time using dark brown paint. Have the children make a print across the top (palm) of their other handprint with fingers together and pointing to the side. When these have dried, the children can add a stem using a brown marker.

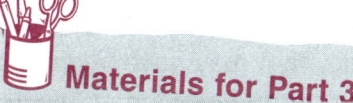

Materials for Part 3:
- *Read to Me Page 81*
- tablecloth and napkins
- sugar cookies
- icing
- candy sprinkles or colored sugar
- juice

Celebrating with My Family (Part 3)

Theme: Jesus took part in family celebrations.

Purpose:
• *to help the children appreciate that Jesus valued celebrations and took part in them.*

Beginning

As the children enter the room, have Sudie Squirrel welcome them. Then help the children find the flowers with their names on them and place them on the tree.

Gather the children in a circle or group. Tell the children that Jesus did things together with his family. They celebrated important events together. Explain that the Holy Family was very much like our families.

Ask the children whether they have ever been to a special celebration with their family that may have taken place at church, such as a wedding or a baptismal ceremony. Tell the children that these two celebrations are usually followed by a party.

Middle

Pass out a copy of *Read to Me Page 81* to each child. Tell the children that this is a story about a special wedding celebration that Jesus went to with his mother, Mary.

Read the story aloud. Ask the children to look at the illustrations as you read the story. Ask the children whether they have heard this story before. Remind them that this is a story that we can read in the Bible.

Tell the children that, by being able to change water into wine, Jesus showed everyone that he was truly the Son of God. God gave Jesus the power to perform miracles. Stress that Jesus was quick to do as his mother asked of him. It was Mary who saw the need for more wine and asked for Jesus' help.

Ask the questions at the end of the story. Invite all the children to share their experiences.

End

Gather the children around the table. Ask whether they remember what special day it is. Tell them that we will now celebrate Sudie's birthday. Encourage the children to help put out the tablecloth and napkins. Have the children bring Sudie her gifts. Give each child a plain sugar cookie. Have the children spread icing on their cookies and decorate them with candy sprinkles or colored sugar. Be sure to have a child decorate a cookie for Sudie. Sing a birthday song to Sudie. Let the children enjoy their cookies with juice. When the celebration is complete, remind the children that they need to help clean up. Involve all the children in this. *Note: Be aware of any children with food allergies before using this activity.*

Gather the children around the prayer table and lead them in the following prayer: "Dear God, thank you for giving us Jesus. Thank you for the gift of celebrations. Amen."

Extra! Extra!

A Special Celebration

Invite the children to act out the wedding at Cana. Provide props for the children to use such as jugs or pitchers, plastic wine glasses, and play food.

 Refer to *Extra! Extra! Page 61* for a related craft activity.

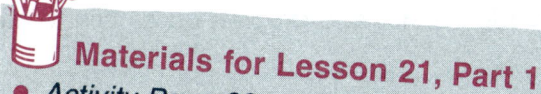

Materials for Lesson 21, Part 1:
● *Activity Page 83*
● vase
● bare branches or sticks

Theme: Jesus wants us to say "I'm sorry."

Purpose:
• *to help the children appreciate the need to say "I'm sorry."*

Beginning

As the children enter the room, have Sudie Squirrel welcome them. Then help the children find the flowers with their names on them and place them on the tree.

Gather the children in a circle on the floor. Remind the children that Jesus wants us to be happy, but he knows and understands it is not always possible. Sometimes unpleasant things happen. Sometimes we are mean and unkind. Reassure the children that when we are unkind, Jesus understands and never stops loving us. He just wants us to say "I'm sorry" and try not to be unkind again.

Act out the following situations with Sudie Squirrel:

• Sudie is holding a nut and drops it on a child. What should Sudie do?

• Have a basket of nuts nearby. Sudie knocks them over. Then have a child pick them up. Sudie knocks them over again. What should Sudie do?

• Sudie takes a toy or crayon away from someone. What should Sudie do?

Invite the children to suggest what Sudie should do in each situation. Lead the children to the conclusion that she should say "I'm sorry."

Middle

Pass out a copy of *Activity Page 83* to each child. Draw the children's attention to the two pictures of the children being unkind. Read aloud the message at the top of the page. Ask the children why the children in these two pictures need to say "I'm sorry." Ask the children whether they have ever experienced an incident at home much like the ones shown on this page.

Ask the children whether there is a family member at home or a friend that needs to hear them say "I'm sorry." Help the children write the card at the bottom of the page to that person. Then let them draw the person in the space provided.

End

Ahead of time, fill a vase with bare branches or sticks, one for each child.

Gather the children in a circle on the floor. Show the children the vase of bare branches. Tell the children that these branches are from a tree, but right now they don't look very good. Explain that we know that branches on a tree have the potential to grow and blossom and look really beautiful. Compare these branches to us. Tell the children that when we are mean, we are like the bare branches: not very pretty. But when we say we are sorry, we grow and blossom and become beautiful people. (Keep the branches at kindergarten for an activity in Part 3 of this lesson.)

Gather the children around the prayer table and lead them in the following prayer: "Dear God, help me to show when I am sorry. Amen."

Extra! Extra!

Make a fish puppet before reading the story *Rainbow Fish to the Rescue* by Marcus Pfister. Paint two large paper plates various colors. Cut out a "V" shape out of each plate for the mouth of the fish. Attach these wedges to the back of the fish to form tails. Glue on squiggly eyes. Decorate with large colorful sequins. Put the two fish together and staple all around, leaving an opening in the bottom for your hand. Use this puppet as you read the story. After reading this story, ask the children what the fish did to act mean. What should the fish have done? How did Rainbow Fish help?

Materials for Part 2:
- *Activity Page 84*
- colored construction paper

Forgiving
(Part 2)

Theme: We show we are sorry by our actions.

Purpose:

• *to develop an awareness in the children of the ways we can show we are sorry.*

Beginning

 As the children enter the room, have Sudie Squirrel welcome them. Then help the children find the flowers with their names on them and place them on the tree.

Gather the children in a circle on the floor. Remind the children that Jesus knows, understands, and forgives each of us. All we have to do is to be really sorry for what we have done and try hard not to do unkind things again.

Teach the children the following song:

♫ **I Am Sorry** *(To the tune of "London Bridge")*

I am sorry, yes I am.
Yes I am, yes I am.
I am sorry, yes I am.
Please forgive me.

Didn't mean to hurt you so,
Hurt you so, hurt you so.
Didn't mean to hurt you so.
I do love you.

Middle

Pass out a copy of *Activity Page 84* to each child. Remind the children that if we have been unkind or mean, we can say we are sorry. Call the children's attention to the illustrations. Begin with the one in the upper left corner of the page. Ask for a volunteer to tell you what is happening in the picture. Follow this same procedure with all the pictures, allowing as many children as possible the opportunity to share. When finished, tell the children to cut out the card and take it home. Give it to someone to show you are sorry.

End

Give each child a piece of colorful construction paper. Have the children trace around their hands with fingers spread wide on this paper. Help the children cut these out. Have the children draw something they have done recently that was mean or unkind. Go around the group and have the children tell you what they have drawn. Write this on their handprints. Keep these handprints at kindergarten for an activity in Part 3 of this lesson.

Gather the children around the prayer table and lead them in the prayer found on the bottom of *Activity Page 84.*

Extra! Extra!

 **Friendly Fish**

Review the story *Rainbow Fish to the Rescue* with the children. Then have the children make paper plate fish puppets. Give each child two large paper plates and have them paint them various colors. Cut out a "V" shape out of each plate for the mouth of the fish. Attach these wedges to the back of the fish to form tails. Glue on squiggly eyes. Give each child one large colorful sequin to glue on his or her fish. Put the two fish together and staple all around, leaving an opening in the bottom for their hands.

 **Materials for Part 3:**
- *Read to Me Page 85*
- vase
- bare branches
- handprints
- floral tape
- pencils

Forgiving
(Part 3)

Theme: When we are sorry God forgives us.

Purpose:
• to help the children learn to forgive and find joy in being forgiven.

Beginning

As the children enter the room, have Sudie Squirrel welcome them. Then help the children find the flowers with their names on them and place them on the tree.

Gather the children in a circle around you. Remind the children that we have been talking about forgiveness. Tell the children that if our hearts are full of love we can easily forgive others who may have been unkind to us. The love that we are talking about is the gift of love that God has given to all of us. We need to learn to use it at all times.

Give the children their handprints we made in Part 2 of this lesson. Ask the children what we can do when we are mean or unkind to someone. Gather the children around the prayer table. Tell them we will ask God for forgiveness. Say the following prayer: "Dear God, I am sorry for being mean and unkind. Help me to always show your love. Amen." Then have each child take a bare branch from the vase. Help the children roll up their handprints and tape the palm part around the stick using floral tape. Roll each "finger" around a pencil to make them curl outwards. Tell the children that the ugly bare branches are now beautiful. Tell the children that we must remember that even when we are mean or unkind, we can be forgiven.

Middle

Pass out a copy of *Read to Me Page 85* to each child. Remind the children that Jesus not only personally showed us how to love and to forgive; he also told us many stories about forgiveness that are recorded in the Bible. Tell the children that on this page is a wonderful story that Jesus told his friends about forgiveness. Invite the children to listen to the story and look at the illustrations as you read the story. When you have finished, remind the children that God always loves us and forgives us when we are sorry. Ask the children the question at the bottom of the page. Let volunteers act out the last two lines.

End

Gather the children in a circle on the floor. Invite several volunteers to act out the story of the prodigal son. Then have the children illustrate this story in their Bible booklets.

Gather the children around the prayer table and lead them in singing the "I Am Sorry" song found on page 142.

Extra! Extra!

How Does It Feel?

Review the story *Rainbow Fish to the Rescue.* Then have the children use the fish puppets they made to act out the story. Use the puppet that you made earlier for the fish that is different. Encourage the children to talk about the feelings of the fish that was left out. How did he feel when the other fish included him?

Materials for Lesson 22, Part 1:
- *Activity Page 87*
- glitter, stickers, paint, and markers
- empty paper towel spools
- white paint
- craft foam
- red, pink, and white crepe paper streamers

Theme: We celebrate the love of God and one another.

Purpose:
• *to help the children appreciate that Valentine's Day is a celebration of love.*

Beginning

As the children enter the room, have Sudie Squirrel welcome them. Then help the children find the flowers with their names on them and place them on the tree.

Gather the children in a circle or group. Tell them that Valentine's Day is near. It is a day set aside to remind us in a special way how much others love us and to show we love them in return. The day is named after Saint Valentine because he loved all of God's people. Remember that when we show our love for others we show love for God.

The heart has been a symbol of love for hundreds of years. This is why we hear people say, "I love you with all my heart!"; "My heart reaches out to you!"; "I give you my heart." Point out that people often express love and appreciation for others by giving them flowers or candy. Ask the children how they show love in their families.

Middle

Pass out a copy of *Activity Page 87* to each child. Read the message on the page to the children. Remind the children that we give valentine cards to tell people we love them.

Have the children decorate the two valentine cards. Provide glitter, stickers, paint, and markers.

End

Gather the children in a circle on the floor. Teach them the following song:

♫ Valentine's Day *(To the tune of "Here We Go Looby-Loo")*

Love is a special gift.
Love is a special gift.
Love is a special gift, gift, gift
That God has given to us.

Love makes us want to dance.
Love makes us want to sing.
Love fills our hearts with joy, joy, joy.
God has been so good to us.

Help the children make "Valentine Wands." Give each child an empty paper towel spool. Have the children paint this white. Give each child a piece of craft foam with a heart drawn on it. Have the children cut out this heart and attach it to the top of the paper towel spool. Attach some red, pink, and white crepe paper streamer to the top of the paper towel spool. Let the children sing the song "Valentine's Day" and dance around with their heart wands.

Gather the children around the prayer table and lead them in the following prayer: "Dear God, thank you for all the people who love us and whom we love. Amen."

Extra! Extra!

 Signs of Love

Help the children make a special valentine for their parents. Give each child a piece of muslin cut into a twelve-inch square. Paint both hands of each child with red or pink paint and "print" them with fingers together on the piece of muslin, overlapping the fingers, to make a heart. Using a permanent marker, write the child's name and the date under the heart. Attach strips of stick-on magnets to the back. Have the children bring these home to say "I love you" to their parents.

 Share the book *Secret Valentine* by Laura Damon with the children.

Jimmy
February 14, _____

 **Materials for Part 2:**
- *Activity Page 88*
- masking tape
- a picture of flowers or real flowers

147

Valentine's Day (Part 2)

Theme: We celebrate the love of God with one another.

Purpose:

• *to help the children appreciate that Valentine's Day is a celebration of love.*

Beginning

As the children enter the room, have Sudie Squirrel welcome them. Then help the children find the flowers with their names on them and place them on the tree.

Make a large heart on the floor using masking tape. Gather the children and have them sit outside of the heart. Remind the children that cards, flowers, and candy are some of the ways people say "I love you," but the best way to say "I love you" is through actions. Ask the children to think of ways they can show love to someone. Then go around the group and give each child a turn to tell some way he or she can show love to someone. After the child has said what he or she could do to show love, have that child come and sit inside the heart. Be sure to give each child an opportunity to share.

Middle

Pass out a copy of *Activity Page 88* to each child. Tell the children that they are going to finish their valentine cards. Read the first four lines on the page. Stress that God will always love us. Ask the children to print their names on the cards where indicated and cut out the cards. When finished, ask the children to whom they will give these valentine cards. Ask what they will say when they deliver them.

End

Make a graph of favorite valentine gifts to give. Use masking tape to make three columns on the floor. Put a picture of valentine candy or a small box of candy in the first column. Put a picture of flowers or some real flowers in the second column. Place a valentine card in the third column. Have the children sit in the column of their favorite valentine gift to give.

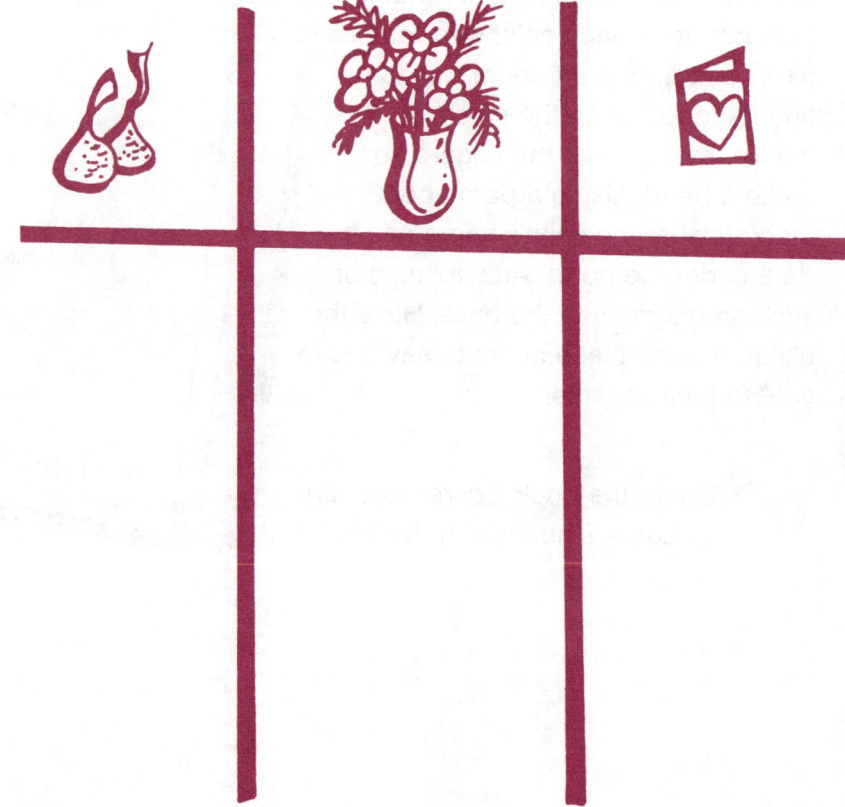

Gather the children around the prayer table. Lead them in the following prayer: "Dear God, please keep our lives full of love so we can share it with others. Amen."

Extra! Extra!

A Bag of Hearts

Help the children make valentine bags. Give each child a large white paper bag. Provide heart-shaped sponges of various sizes and trays of red, pink, and purple paint. Let the children sponge hearts all over their bags. Allow to dry. Keep these in kindergarten to put valentine treats in.

Materials for Part 3:
- *Read to Me* Page 89
- a Valentine Mailbox made from a shoebox and colorful paper
- craftfoam
- popsicle sticks
- 4" by 6" index cards or tagboard
- heart-shaped stickers
- heart-shaped bread slices
- cream cheese, grape or strawberry jam
- juice
- construction paper
- variously-sized cans
- red, pink, and white spray paint
- wrapped candies

Valentine's Day
(Part 3)

Theme: We show our love on Valentine's Day and every day.

Purpose:
- *to encourage the children to discover ways they can show their love each day, not just on Valentine's Day.*

Beginning
Ahead of time prepare a "Valentine Mailbox." Take a large shoe box and cover it with colorful paper. Cut around the top and sides of one small side so that this "mailbox" can be opened like a rural mailbox. Attach a red heart cut from craft foam to a popsicle stick. Attach this to the side of the "mailbox" to resemble the flag on a rural mailbox.

As the children enter the room, have Sudie Squirrel welcome them. Then help the children find the flowers with their names on them and place them on the tree.

Help the children make valentines for their preschool friends. Give each child a 4" by 6" index card or a piece of tagboard cut to that size. On one side write: *Happy Valentine's Day! From _____ (child's name)*. (Note: Do not write "To," as these cards will be chosen later at random.) Provide heart-shaped stickers for decorations. Have the children "mail" these cards in the mailbox.

Middle
Pass out a copy of *Read to Me Page 89* to each child. Remind the children that we have been talking about the many ways we share Jesus' love, and that Valentine's Day is a special time set aside to celebrate that love.

Read aloud "On Valentine's Day." Read the questions at the end of the poem. Invite all the children into the discussion. Conclude by telling the children that love should be shown all year.

End
Have a valentine celebration with the children. Prepare three centers and move around them with the children.

The first center is a snack center. Help the children make heart-shaped bread by cutting into a slice of bread with a heart-shaped cookie cutter. Then let the children spread softened cream cheese on the bread. Give them a choice of grape or strawberry jam to top off their cream cheese. Serve juice.

In the second center, the children will make heart headbands. Cut strips of construction paper and staple to fit around each child's head. Then provide construction paper hearts in various colors and sizes. Have the children decorate their headbands by gluing several hearts on them. Heart-shaped stickers can also be added.

Play a "Can-dee" game. Spraypaint cans of various sizes and heights red, pink, and white. Give each child a handful of wrapped candies. Have the children take turns standing over the cans and dropping their candies into the cans.

Gather the children around the prayer table and lead them in the following prayer: "Dear God, help me to love as Jesus showed us and to put our love into words and actions. Amen."

Hand out the valentine cards made at the beginning of this lesson.

Extra! Extra!

 Read the book *Bee My Valentine* by Miriam Cohen.

Materials for Lesson 23, Part 1:
- *Activity Page 91*
- pictures of representations of new life
- masking tape
- small blankets or towels
- plastic eggs
- crinkled paper
- small pom-poms
- orange construction paper

Theme: We see signs of new life in the spring.

Purpose:
• *to provide experiences from which the children can discover and identify signs of new life we see in the spring.*

Beginning

As the children enter the room, have Sudie Squirrel welcome them. Then help the children find the flowers with their names on them and place them on the tree.

Gather the children in a circle or group. Remind the children that we are now in the spring season. It is the perfect time to celebrate Easter. Everything is so alive. Show them pictures of the new life we see in spring: bulbs and flowers in a garden, baby chickens being born, frogs on a rock near a pond, birds building a nest, butterflies, buds on trees. Take the children for a walk outside. Help them find signs of new life.

Play an "Eggs Hatching in the Nest" game with the children. Make a large circle on the floor with masking tape. Have the children sit in this "nest" and cover themselves with towels or small blankets. Sing the following song, having the children act it out.

🎵 **Eggs in a Nest** *(To the tune of "Twinkle, Twinkle, Little Star")*

Tiny eggs in a round brown nest
Do not move, just seem to rest.
Is there something in your shell?

Are you empty? I can't tell.
Tap, tap, crack, crack, peep, peep, peep!
Look, a chick awake from sleep!

Middle

Pass out a copy of *Activity Page 91* to each child. Point out the Easter scene at the top of the page. Ask why this is a sign of Easter.

Tell the children that this page has a hidden puzzle and in the hidden puzzle are pictures of live plants and birds and animals. Ask whether they can find them. Ask for volunteers to tell you what they have found. When each living thing has been named and located, have the children color it. Then ask the children whether they know where these things come from.

End

Make a "Baby Bird Nest" with the children. Give each child half of a plastic egg. Have them fill this egg with crinkled paper or straw to make a nest. Explain that birds build nests in trees to lay their eggs in. The nest cushions the eggs. The eggs stay in the nest until the baby bird is born. Give each child two small pom-poms to glue together to make a bird. Add a triangle of orange construction paper for a beak and two squiggly eyes. Place these "chicks" in the nests.

Gather the children around the prayer table and lead them in the following prayer: "Thank you, God, for the spring season; for the many flowers that bloom; for the newborn animals; for all our gifts of new life. Amen."

Extra! Extra!

Fine Feathered Nest

Give each child a packaged shortcake. Have them spoon in prepared whipped topping to make the cushioning of the nest. Fill with jelly bean eggs.

Read the book *My First Easter* by Tomie dePaola.

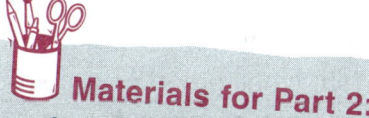

Materials for Part 2:
- *Activity Page 92*
- spring-type clothespins
- small green pom-poms
- children's Bible
- yarn
- six-inch squares of fabric

Easter
(Part 2)

Theme: We learn some of the Christian symbols of Easter.

Purpose:
• *to help the children identify and enjoy some of the traditional symbols associated with our celebration of Easter.*

Beginning

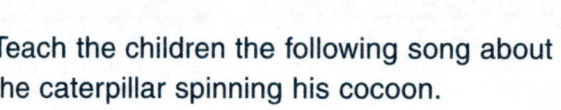 As the children enter the room, have Sudie Squirrel welcome them. Then help the children find the flowers with their names on them and place them on the tree.

Gather the children. Tell them that we see many butterflies in the spring. Ask the children whether they know where butterflies come from. Lead them to discover that caterpillars build cocoons and, after many days, emerge as beautiful butterflies.

Make caterpillars with the children. Give each child a spring-type clothespin and four small green pom-poms. Help the children glue these pom-poms in a line on the clothespin.

Teach the children the following song about a caterpillar:

♫ Creeping, Crawling Caterpillar *(To the tune of "Twinkle, Twinkle, Little Star")*

Creeping, crawling, on a tree,
Eating every leaf I see,
I'm a caterpillar small,
Being careful not to fall.
Creeping, crawling, on a tree,
Eating every leaf I see.

Gather the children in a circle or group. Read from a children's Bible or tell in your own words the story of the passion and death of Jesus (Matthew 27:27–66). Explain to the children that the cocoons that we will place around our caterpillars remind us of the place where Jesus' body was buried.

Middle
Pass out a copy of *Activity Page 92* to each child. Read the first lines to the children. Draw their attention to the Easter symbols and objects on the page. Discuss them together. Be sure to point out that they are signs of Jesus' new life at Easter. Have the children cut these out, punch holes at the tops, and thread a piece of yarn or string through the holes. Hang them on the tree with the children's names or on a Friendship Tree in the room.

End

 Give each child a six-inch square piece of fabric. Let the children decorate this fabric with paint. When dry, have the children wrap their caterpillars in this fabric to make a cocoon.

Teach the children the following song about the caterpillar spinning his cocoon.

♫ Spinning a Cocoon *(To the tune of "Twinkle, Twinkle, Little Star")*

Spinning, spinning, round
  and round,
Making a cocoon of brown.
Inside I will take a rest

Like an egg lying in its nest.
Spinning, spinning, round
  and round,
Making a cocoon of brown.

 Gather the children around the prayer table and lead them in the prayer found on the bottom of *Activity Page 92*.

154

Extra! Extra!

 Read the book *Corduroy's Easter* by Don Freeman.

 Easter

(To the tune of "Frère Jacques")

Spring is here now.
Spring is here now.
Seeds will grow.
Flowers bloom.
God gives us our new life.
God gives us our new life.
Easter's here.
Easter's here.

Alleluia!
Alleluia!
Celebrate!
Celebrate!
Jesus Christ is risen.
Jesus Christ is risen.
Easter joy!
Easter joy!

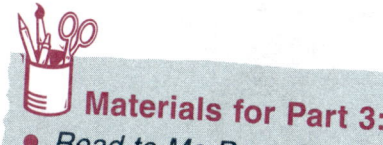 **Materials for Part 3:**
- *Read to Me* Page 93
- small blankets or towels

155

Easter (Part 3)

Theme: We celebrate the coming of Easter.

Purpose:
• *to help the children experience the joy of Easter morning.*

Beginning

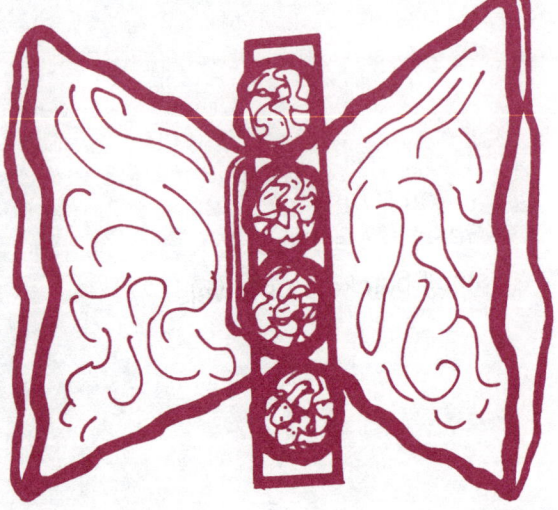 As the children enter the room, have Sudie Squirrel welcome them. Then help the children find the flowers with their names on them and place them on the tree.

Have the children remove the cocoons from their caterpillars. Gather the painted fabric in the center and insert into the clothespin to make butterfly wings. Tell the children that the caterpillars have now emerged from their cocoons and turned into beautiful butterflies.

Teach the children the following song about a butterfly coming out of its cocoon:

♫ Pretty Butterfly *(To the tune of "Twinkle, Twinkle, Little Star")*

Out of my cocoon I fly,
I'm a pretty butterfly.
I once looked like I was dead.
Surprise! I now have wings to spread.
Out of my cocoon I fly,
I'm a pretty butterfly.

Middle

Pass out a copy of *Read to Me Page 93* to each child. Invite the children to look at the pictures which surround the story. Read the page to the children. When finished, have volunteers come up and act out how the baby chick, the butterfly, and the flower have new life. Then invite children to share how their families celebrate Easter. Ask children why Easter is the best celebration. Lead the children to conclude that, at Easter, Jesus has new life and he shares this new life with us.

End

Gather the children in a circle on the floor. Provide each child with a towel or small blanket. Tell the children that we will act out changing from a caterpillar to a butterfly. Sing the three songs beginning with "Creeping, Crawling Caterpillar." Have the children act out each stage, using their towels or blankets as cocoons and then as butterfly wings.

Gather the children around the prayer table. Lead them in the following prayer: "Dear Jesus, thank you for giving us new life and for being with us always. Amen."

Extra! Extra!

 **A Caterpillar-to-Butterfly Snack**

Give each child a gummy worm. Tell them that this is the caterpillar. Then give each child a colorful rolled-up fruit snack. Have the children roll their "caterpillars" up in this to make a cocoon. Then, when the butterfly comes out of the cocoon, have the children gather the rolled-up fruit snack in the center and pinch it. Candy wafers or other colorful candies can be placed on the rolled-up fruit snack to decorate the wings. Place the gummy worm in the center of the rolled-up fruit snack to make a butterfly. Sing the songs as the children go from stage to stage. Then let the children eat their sign of new life. *Note: Be aware of any children with food allergies before using this activity.*

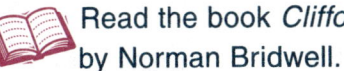 Read the book *Clifford's Happy Easter* by Norman Bridwell.

 **Materials for Lesson 24, Part 1:**
- *Activity Page 95*
- children's Bible
- real candle, bushel basket
- empty toilet paper spools
- yellow craft foam

157

Theme: From the Bible, we learn more about God and God's Son, Jesus.

Purpose:

• *to help the children appreciate that in the Bible we read about Jesus Christ, God's own Son.*

Beginning

As the children enter the room, have Sudie Squirrel welcome them. Then help the children find the flowers with their names on them and place them on the tree.

Gather the children in a circle on the floor. Show them the children's Bible. Remind the children that the Bible was written by people who lived many, many years ago. These people wanted to write about God and his Son, Jesus, so that other people could come to learn about God's greatest gift to us, Jesus Christ.

Tell the children that we will read from our Bible today. Read from a children's Bible or tell in your own words the passage from Matthew 5:14–16, "Let Your Light Shine." To enhance the experience, use props such as a real candle and a basket.

Have the children illustrate this reading in their Bible story booklets.

Middle

Pass out a copy of *Activity Page 95* to each child. Point out the picture of the woman reading the Bible to a child. Ask the children whether they like to be read to.

Read aloud the words at the top of the page. Then have the children look at the picture of the sun. Tell the children that the bright sun reminds us of Jesus. Call the children's attention to the candle. Explain that there is a candle like this one in our church. It also reminds us of Jesus. Invite the children to color the sun and the candle.

End

Help the children make "candles." Give each child an empty toilet paper spool. Have them paint these white. Cut a flame shape from yellow craft foam and attach to the top of the toilet paper spool. Then let the children use these as they sing the following song:

🎵 **Let It Shine** *(To the tune of "Mary Had a Little Lamb")*

Hide it under a bushel? No!
A bushel? No.
A bushel? No.
Hide it under a bushel? No!
Let it shine, let it shine.

Gather the children around the prayer table and lead them in the following prayer: "Dear God, thank you for giving us your special book, the Bible, so that we may learn about your Son, Jesus. Amen."

Extra! Extra!

Our Shining Lights

Provide a large rectangular piece of styrofoam. Have the children stick their candles made in the **End** of this lesson in the styrofoam. Place this in the window or on the prayer table so that all may see how we let our lights shine.

 Read the book *The Lonely Firefly* by Eric Carle.

Materials for Part 2:
- *Activity Page 96*
- children's Bible
- tongue depressors
- small strips of cloth
- non-spring clothespins

More About the Bible
(Part 2)

Theme: In the Bible, Jesus shows us how to love.

Purpose:
• *to make the children aware of the way the Bible teaches us of Jesus' love.*

Beginning
As the children enter the room, have Sudie Squirrel welcome them. Then help the children find the flowers with their names on them and place them on the tree.

Gather the children in a circle on the floor. Show them the Bible. Tell the children that today we will read another story from the Bible. Read from a children's Bible or tell in your own words the story of Jesus healing the lepers (Luke 17:11–19). To enhance the experience, use ten tongue depressors with faces drawn on them to represent the ten lepers. Use ten small strips of cloth to wrap the lepers in. When they are healed, take off the strips of cloth. Stress that only one came back to thank Jesus.

Have the children illustrate this story in their Bible story booklets.

Middle
Pass out a copy of *Activity Page 96* to each child. Call the children's attention to the Bible frame. Read the Bible verse from John. Invite the children to draw a picture of Jesus and themselves doing a loving action for someone.

End
Give each child a non-spring type of clothespin. Have the children draw a face on the rounded part. Then give each child a small strip of fabric. Explain that the lepers were very contagious, so they had to stay wrapped up in bandages so as not to let their disease spread. Have the children act out the story using their clothespins. Tell the children that they have only one clothespin to remind them to be like the one leper who came back to thank Jesus. We must always thank Jesus for our wonderful gifts.

Gather the children around the prayer table. Lead them in the prayer found on the top of *Activity Page 96.*

160

Extra! Extra!

 Thank You Very Much!

Remind the children that it is important to give thanks to God and to others. Help the children make a thank-you card for someone who has done something nice for them. Give each child a 4" by 6" piece of tagboard. Write the word *Thanks* on each one. Let the children use various art materials to decorate their cards. Encourage the children to give these cards to someone who has done something nice for them.

Materials for Part 3:
- towels, bandages
- candle, bushel basket
- creme-filled yellow snack cakes
- yellow gel icing

More About the Bible (Part 3)

Theme: In the Bible we read about Jesus.

Purpose:
• *to provide early learning experiences for the children's appreciation of the Bible.*

Beginning

 As the children enter the room, have Sudie Squirrel welcome them. Then help the children find the flowers with their names on them and place them on the tree.

Gather the children in a circle on the floor. Review the two readings from the Bible in this lesson. Then invite volunteers to come and act out the story of Jesus healing the lepers. Provide props such as towels for the bandages for the children to use.

Then act out the "let your light shine" reading. Let the children act this out by going under the tables when the candle is hidden under a bushel.

Middle
Let the children make an "Edible Candle." Give each child a cream-filled yellow snack cake on a paper plate. Have them draw the flame of the candle using yellow gel icing. Then have them add red cinnamon candies to the flame. Let the children enjoy their snacks. *Note: Be aware of any children with food allergies before using this activity.*

End
To conclude this unit, take down all the spring decorations around the room. Give the children the flowers with their names on them to take home. Explain to the children that when they come back to kindergarten, they will have something new with their names on them to hang on our tree.

Lead the children in the following prayer: "Dear God, help us to follow Jesus and let our lights shine. Amen."

Extra! Extra!

Bible Booklets

Give the children their Bible story booklets. Have them look through and recall all the stories we learned. Then have the children select one as their favorite. Give each child a piece of paper. Have the children illustrate their favorite readings from the Bible. Add these pages to their booklets.

Materials for *Summer Unit Page*:

- *Unit Page 97*
- green leaf for each child
- summer items such as a bathing suit, a suitcase, a globe, a camera, a pail and shovel, a beachball, sunglasses, suntan lotion, and so on
- empty paper towel spools
- brown paint
- green tissue paper
- sugar cookies
- popsicle sticks or plastic knives
- green icing
- green candy-coated chocolates or other green candies
- chocolate-covered cookie sticks
- lemonade

Theme: Celebrating Summer

Beginning

A small tree should be attached to the wall at the children's eye level. Prepare a leaf from green construction paper for each child with his or her name on it. As each child enters the preschool room, he or she should find the leaf with his or her name on it and attach it to the tree.

Introduce the season of summer by bringing in items that are particular to this time of year. Some items might include a bathing suit, a suitcase, a globe, a camera, a pail and shovel, a beach ball, sunglasses, suntan lotion, a baseball and mitt, shorts, and so on. Gather the children and show them these objects. Talk about the season of summer. Explain that the leaves on the trees are green and some trees have beautiful flowers on them. The weather gets very hot.

Teach the children the following song:

♪ Summer's Coming (To the tune of "Frère Jacques")

**Summer's coming, summer's coming.
Trips we'll take, trips we'll take.
Ice cream and picnics; ice cream and picnics!
Celebrate! Celebrate!**

Middle

Pass out a copy of the *Unit Page* to each child. Explain that the pictures show people having fun doing things in the summer. Invite the children to make up a story about each picture. Ask the children what they like to do in the summer.

End

Make a summer tree. Give each child an empty paper towel spool. Have the children paint this brown. Cut several slits in the top and bend the strips outward to form branches. Have the children put a thin layer of glue on these branches. Give the children green tissue paper squares. Show them how to crumple the tissue squares and stick them onto the glue-covered branches.

Make "Super Summer Trees" together. Give each child a round sugar cookie. Have the children use popsicle sticks or plastic knives to cover this with green icing. Give the children green candy-coated chocolates or other green candies to put on top of the icing. Give each child a rectangular chocolate-covered cookie stick to use as a tree trunk. Enjoy with lemonade. *Note: Be aware of any children with food allergies before using this activity.*

Extra! Extra!

 A Handprint Summer Tree

Paint each child's forearm brown (the tree-trunk) and stamp this onto a piece of light blue construction paper. Paint the child's hand (with fingers open wide) green. Help the child stamp this at the top of the trunk to complete the tree.

 Read any of the following books:

The Best Vacation Ever, written by Stuart J. Murphy, published by HarperCollins Children's Books (New York) 1997.

Beach Feet, written by Lynn Reiser, published by Greenwillow Books (New York) 1996.

When Daddy Took Us Camping, written by Julie Brillhart, published by Albert Whitman & Company (Morton Grove, IL) 1997.

When Summer Comes, written by Robert Maass, published by Henry Holt and Company, 1996.

Additional Suggestions for Storytime During Unit 4

Bridges, Margaret Park. *If I Were Your Mother.* New York: Morrow Junior Books, 1999.

Bunting, Eve. *The Mother's Day Mice.* Boston: Houghton Mifflin Company, 1988.

_____. *A Perfect Father's Day.* Boston: Houghton Mifflin, 1993.

Carle, Eric. *Papa, Please Get the Moon for Me.* New York: Simon & Schuster Children's Publishing, 1991.

Caswell, Helen Rayburn. *I Can Talk to God.* Nashville, TN: Abingdon Press, 1996.

Cowen-Fletcher, Jane. *Mama Zooms.* New York: Scholastic, Inc., 1996.

Daly-Weir, Catherine. *Daddy and Me.* New York: Penguin Putnam Books for Young Readers, 1999.

Flack, Marjorie. *Ask Mr. Bear.* Pine Plains, NY: Live Oak Media, 1991.

Gardella, Tricia. *Just Like My Dad.* New York: HarperCollins Children's Books, 1996.

Grambling, Lois G. *Daddy Will Be There.* New York: Greenwillow Books, 1998.

Joosse, Barbara M. *Mama, Do You Love Me?* San Francisco, CA: Chronicle Books, 1991.

King, Stephen Michael. *A Special Kind of Love.* New York: Scholastic, Inc., 1996.

Numeroff, Laura. *What Daddies Do Best.* New York: Simon & Schuster, 1998.

_____. *What Mommies Do Best.* New York: Simon & Schuster, 1998.

Porter-Gaylord, Laurel. *I Love My Daddy Because . . .* New York: Putnam Publishing Group, 1991.

Rosenberg, Liz. *Monster Mama.* New York: Putnam Publishing Group, 1997.

Smalls, Irene. *Jonathan and His Mommy.* New York: Little Brown & Company, 1994.

Staenberg, Bonnie. *A Present for Mama Bear.* New York: Scholastic, Inc., 1999.

Tafuri, Nancy. *I Love You, Little One.* New York: Scholastic, Inc., 1998.

 **Materials for Lesson 25, Part 1:**
- *Activity Page 99*
- large pillar-shaped candle
- fabric paint

Theme: We explore what Baptism means in our lives.

Purpose:
• *to deepen the children's awareness that through Baptism they became members of a special family, the Catholic Church.*

Beginning

As the children enter the room, have Sudie Squirrel welcome them. Then help the children find the leaves with their names on them and place them on the tree.

Gather the children in a circle on the floor. Remind the children that we learned about the sacrament of Baptism. Ask the children whether they can remember when we pretended to baptize a baby doll. Show pictures if available. Ask the children to recall the experience. What was done? What was used?

Sing the song "I Am Growing" from Lesson 11, page 82, with the children.

Middle

Pass out a copy of *Activity Page 99* to each child. Draw the children's attention to the baptismal picture. Discuss who is present. Stress that the baby being baptized will become a member of a special family, the Catholic Church. Point out the candle. Ask the children what some other signs of Baptism are (baptismal garment, water).

Read aloud the message at the top of the page. Have the children print their names vertically on the baptismal candle. Help as needed.

End

Help the children to make a prayer candle for the prayer table. Provide a large pillar-shaped candle. Make a cross on the candle using the children's thumbprints. Have each child dip his or her thumb in fabric paint and press one print on the candle. Help the children put their prints in the shape of a cross. Remind the children that when they were baptized, they became members of a special family, the Catholic Church. The cross is a sign to show we are members of this special family.

Gather the children around the prayer table and lead them in the following prayer: "Dear God, thank you for welcoming us into a special family, the Catholic Church, when we were baptized. Amen."

Extra! Extra!

 Baptism Cards

Help the children make prayer cards to place on their prayer tables at home. Give each child a 3" by 5" index card or piece of tagboard. Have each glue a birthday candle on this card. Write their names across the top of the cards. On the bottom of the cards write the words *A Child of God.* Tell the children that this will remind them that at Baptism they received the light of Christ and became children of God.

Laurie

A Child of God

Materials for Part 2:
- *Activity Page 100*
- large sheet of white bulletin board paper
- paint

Loving God
(Part 2)

Theme: We respond to Jesus' invitation to be his friends.

Purpose:

• *to help the children begin to develop an appreciation of the joy and meaning of the celebration of Baptism.*

Beginning

As the children enter the room, have Sudie Squirrel welcome them. Then help the children find the leaves with their names on them and place them on the tree.

Gather the children in a circle on the floor. Teach them the following song:

♫ My Baptism *(To the tune of "Mary Had a Little Lamb")*

I became a child of God,
Child of God, child of God.
I became a child of God
On my Baptism day.

Jesus said, "Come, follow me,
Follow me, follow me."
Jesus said, "Come, follow me"
On my Baptism day.

Play a "Follow the Leader" game with the children. Select one child to be the "leader" and have the other children do whatever that child does. Give each child a turn to be the leader. Explain that just as the leader in the game showed us what to do, Jesus shows us how to live our lives.

Middle

Pass out a copy of *Activity Page 100.* Read aloud the message at the top of the page. Talk about some of the ways Jesus shows us how to live in God's family and in our own families, too. Point out the quotation from Scripture at the bottom of the page. Explain that Jesus says, "Come and be my friend." Ask the children what they think Jesus means. Point out that it is not always easy to be a follower of Jesus, and Jesus knows this. Jesus just wants us to keep trying and always to do our best. Jesus is always with us, helping us to live as children of God. Have the children color the baptismal candle and cut it out.

End

Spread out a large sheet of white bulletin board paper on the floor. (If weather permits, do this activity outside.) Have the children take off their shoes and socks. Paint the bottoms of their feet and have them walk across the paper leaving a colored footprint trail. Write across the top of the paper: *We Follow Jesus.* When dry, hang this in the room.

Gather the children around the prayer table and lead them in prayer: "Thank you, Jesus, for calling us to be your friends. Amen."

Extra! Extra!

The End-of-Year Scrapbook

Make scrapbook pages for the children's scrapbooks. Paint the children's feet and have them make a single set of footprints on a piece of construction paper. Write across the top of the page the words *I follow Jesus.* Add this page to the others in the children's scrapbooks.

Materials for Part 3:

• *Read to Me Page 101*
• construction paper
• yellow paint and blue paint
• small pieces of white fabric
• marker

Loving God
(Part 3)

Theme: We learn to live as members of the Christian family.

Purpose:
• *to assist the children in becoming aware of how happy their own families and their parish family were when they were baptized.*

Beginning
As the children enter the room, have Sudie Squirrel welcome them. Then help the children find the leaves with their names on them and place them on the tree.

Take the children to the parish church. As the children enter the church, show them how to dip their fingers into the holy water near the door and make the sign of the cross. Making the sign of the cross with holy water reminds us of our Baptism. It reminds us that we belong to the Catholic Church. Show the children the baptismal font. Explain that this is where babies and people of all ages are baptized and welcomed into the Church family.

Middle
Pass out a copy of *Read to Me Page 101* to each child. Tell the children that this story is about a particular Baptism celebration, much like theirs. Draw the children's attention to the illustrations. Point out how happy everyone seems.

Now read the story aloud. Ask the questions at the end of the story. Involve all the children in the discussion.

End
Give each child a piece of construction paper. Help the children fold this in three sections. Then unfold. Tell the children that we will put the symbols of Baptism on this paper. In the first section, have the children draw a rectangle for a candle. Then have them fingerprint a yellow flame on this candle.

For the second section, give each child a small piece of white fabric. Have them glue this to their papers. Then have them use a marker to make a cross on the fabric. Explain that this represents the special baptismal garment that they wore when they were baptized.

In the third section of their papers, have the children illustrate water by making blue fingerprint water drops.

Gather the children around the prayer table and lead them in the following prayer: "Dear God, it is so wonderful to be your child. Thank you for all of your gifts. Amen." Conclude by singing the song "My Baptism" found on page 168.

Extra! Extra!

 ## Jesus Sends the Disciples to Baptize

Gather the children in a circle on the floor. Tell them that Jesus sent his disciples (his special followers) to baptize in the name of the Father, and of the Son, and of the Holy Spirit. Invite the children to make the sign of the cross with you. Then read from a children's Bible or tell in your own words the story of Jesus' commissioning of the disciples (Matthew 28:16–20). To enhance the experience, prepare pictures from the story on tagboard, color, and cut out. Attach a piece of sticky velcro to the back and put on a carpet square as you read or tell the story.

After telling this story, invite the children to act it out. Then have them illustrate this story in their Bible story booklets.

 ## A Baptism Cross

To remind the children of Baptism, give each of them a piece of construction paper with a cross already drawn on it. Invite them to decorate their crosses with crayons, markers, or other craft materials. You may want to have the children add fingerprint "water drops" at random around the cross, using blue paint or a blue stamp pad, to emphasize the theme of Baptism.

Materials for Lesson 26, Part 1:

- *Activity Page 103*
- construction paper, glue
- air-dry clay
- markers
- toothpick
- yarn or ribbon

Theme: We learn to love God and others.

Purpose:
• *to encourage the children's growing awareness of God's loving presence.*

Beginning

As the children enter the room, have Sudie Squirrel welcome them. Then help the children find the leaves with their names on them and place them on the tree.

Gather the children in a circle on the floor. Show the children a cross. Pass it among the children. Point out how a cross is made—a long bar and a short one intersecting. Remind the children that a cross is a sign that shows we are Christians.

Ask the children whether they can remember where they have seen a cross. Take the children for a walk around the building, looking for crosses. Take the children into church—are there any crosses there? Ask the children what they think of when they see a cross.

Middle

Pass out a copy of *Activity Page 103* to each child. Read aloud the first five lines on the page. Let the children decorate the crosses on their pages using various colors of construction paper. Have the children spread glue on the cross and then tear off small pieces of construction paper and put them on the glue. The children should cover their crosses with the colored paper.

End

Help the children make crosses to wear. Give each child a small amount of air-dry clay. Show the children how to roll this into two "snakes" and to make these into a cross. Invite the children to decorate these crosses using markers. Use a toothpick to poke a hole in the top of the cross. Thread a piece of yarn or ribbon through this hole and tie to make a necklace. Tell the children to wear their crosses as a sign of God's love.

Gather the children around the prayer table. Lead them in the following prayer: "Dear Jesus, thank you for teaching us how to live as God's children. Amen."

Extra! Extra!

A Cross Shape

Give each child a paper plate and two cookie sticks. Have the children arrange the cookie sticks in the shape of a cross on the plate. Then let the children eat and enjoy them.

Note: Be aware of any children with food allergies before using this activity.

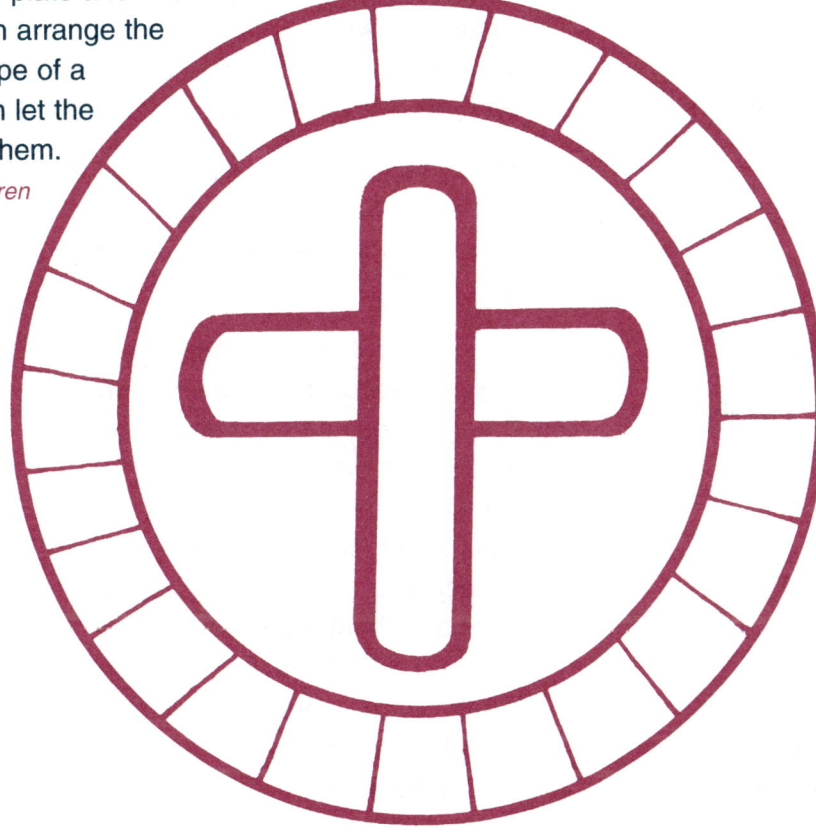

Materials for Part 2:
- *Activity Page 104*
- Bible
- large cross made from cardboard or poster board

173

Knowing God (Part 2)

Theme: We learn to love others as we love ourselves.

Purpose:

• *to deepen the children's relationship with Jesus, who shows us how to love God and others.*

Beginning

As the children enter the room, have Sudie Squirrel welcome them. Then help the children find the leaves with their names on them and place them on the tree.

Gather the children in a circle on the floor. Read the following poem to them:

The Bible

The B-I-B-L-E (*Spell out each letter.*)
Opens up the key,
So everyone can see
How God loves you and me.

Explain to the children that the Bible is an important source of help in living as children of God. Read Matthew 22:37,39 to the children. Tell the children that in the Bible we read that Jesus told us to love God with all our hearts, and to love our neighbors as ourselves. Ask the children whether they know what Jesus meant by this.

You can help develop this understanding by asking this kind of question: "Would you want someone to push you down on the playground?" When the children respond negatively, say, "Then we shouldn't do it to others. This is what Jesus meant."

Middle

Pass out a copy of *Activity Page 104* to each child. Tell the children to look closely at their crosses. Each one has printed on it Jesus' message of love that we just read from the Bible. Read it aloud for the children. Discuss what it means in terms of their everyday life experiences.

Then read aloud the message at the top of the page. Have the children color their crosses and cut them out. Show the children how to fold the papers to make the crosses stand up.

End

Make a large cross from a piece of cardboard or poster board. Cut this cross into puzzle pieces, having one piece for each child in the group. Give each child a piece to the puzzle and have them draw a heart on it. Then have the children put the puzzle together. Explain that showing love to others is one way we show love to God.

Gather the children around the prayer table and lead them in the following prayer: "Dear God, help us to grow in your love. Amen."

Extra! Extra!

Love in Action

Allow the children time to enjoy free play in the room. Put out blocks, puzzles, and art supplies. Open the home center. Tell the children that they have many chances to show love to their neighbors when they play. Ask the children whether they know what this means. Explain that they can show love by sharing, taking turns, helping each other, and playing nicely. Invite the children to find something to play with, reminding them to show love to their neighbors as they play.

Materials for Part 3:
- *Read to Me Page 105*
- children's Bible
- pictures on tagboard
- velcro
- carpet square
- strips of white construction paper
- pink paint and sponges

Knowing God
(Part 3)

Theme: We believe in Jesus' friendship and love.

Purpose:

• to help the children appreciate that God will always love and treasure them.

Beginning

As the children enter the room, have Sudie Squirrel welcome them. Then help the children find the leaves with their names on them and place them on the tree.

Gather the children in a circle or group. Tell the children that we will learn about God's great love for us from another story in the Bible. Explain that Jesus told this story to show how much God loves each one of us and how each one of us is special. Tell the story of the Good Shepherd (Matthew 18:12–14; Luke 15:3–7; or John 10:14–18) in your own words or read from a children's Bible. To enhance the experience, prepare pictures from the story on tagboard, color, and cut out. Attach a piece of sticky velcro to the back and put on a carpet square as you read or tell the story.

Middle

Pass out a copy of *Read to Me Page 105* to each child. Have the children look at the illustrations as you read the story aloud. Ask the questions at the end of the story. Encourage all the children to participate in the discussion.

End

Have the children make sheep headbands. Cut strips of white construction paper and staple to fit around each child's head. Draw two ears on white construction paper for each child and have them cut these out. Attach these to the headbands. Let the children sponge paint pink inside the ears. Have the children put the headbands on. Select one child to be the Good Shepherd. Have the children act out the story of the Good Shepherd.

Have the children illustrate this story in their Bible booklets.

Gather the children around the prayer table and lead them in the following prayer: "Dear God, thank you for your love and care. Amen."

Extra! Extra!

A Sheep to Eat

Make edible sheep for the children to enjoy. Give each child a large paper plate and four cookie sticks. Have the children arrange the cookie sticks on their plates to resemble a sheep's legs. Go around the group and squirt whipped cream over the top of the cookie sticks to make the sheep's body. Then have the children use a round chocolate mint candy to make the face of the sheep. Let the children enjoy their snacks.

Note: Be aware of any children with food allergies before using this activity.

Materials for Lesson 27, Part 1:
- *Activity Page 107*
- small votive candle for each child
- fabric paint

177

Theme: We talk and listen to one another.

Purpose:
• *to help the children recall their own experiences of talking and listening.*

Beginning

As the children enter the room, have Sudie Squirrel welcome them. Then help the children find the leaves with their names on them and place them on the tree.

Gather the children in a circle or group. Have Sudie Squirrel go around the circle and have a short conversation with each child. Explain to the children that it is easy to talk to Sudie Squirrel. Ask the children who else they like to talk to. Lead the children to the conclusion that we talk to friends and family members that we care about and who care about us. Tell the children that we also talk to God. Explain that each time we gather around the prayer table to pray, we are really just talking to God. We talk to God because we love God and have things we want to say to him.

Teach the children the following song:

♪ **I'm Learning How to Pray** *(To the tune of "Go 'Round the Village")*

**I'm learning how to pray,
I'm learning how to pray,
I'm learning how to pray,
'Cause I'm a child of God.**

**Jesus taught me how to pray,
He taught me how to pray,
Yes, he taught me how to pray,
'Cause I'm a child of God.**

Middle

Pass out a copy of *Activity Page 107* to each child. Draw the children's attention to the illustrations. Ask them to look very closely at the pictures beginning with the picture on the top left. Ask what the children are doing. To whom are they listening? Who is reading to them? What do they think she is reading?

Follow the same procedure with each of the other illustrations. Explain to the children that, in each of these pictures, talking and listening is important.

End

Give each child a small votive candle. Provide fabric paint. Encourage the children to decorate their candles with their fingerprints made from the fabric paint. Tell the children to bring these candles home to put on their prayer tables.

Gather the children around the prayer table and lead them in the following prayer: "Dear God, help us always to listen to you. Amen."

Extra! Extra!

Candle-Drippers

Give each child a small paper plate. Provide paints and markers. Encourage the children to decorate their plates as they wish. Then have the children bring these plates home and give their plate to their parents. The plate may be put under a candle holder and placed on their prayer table.

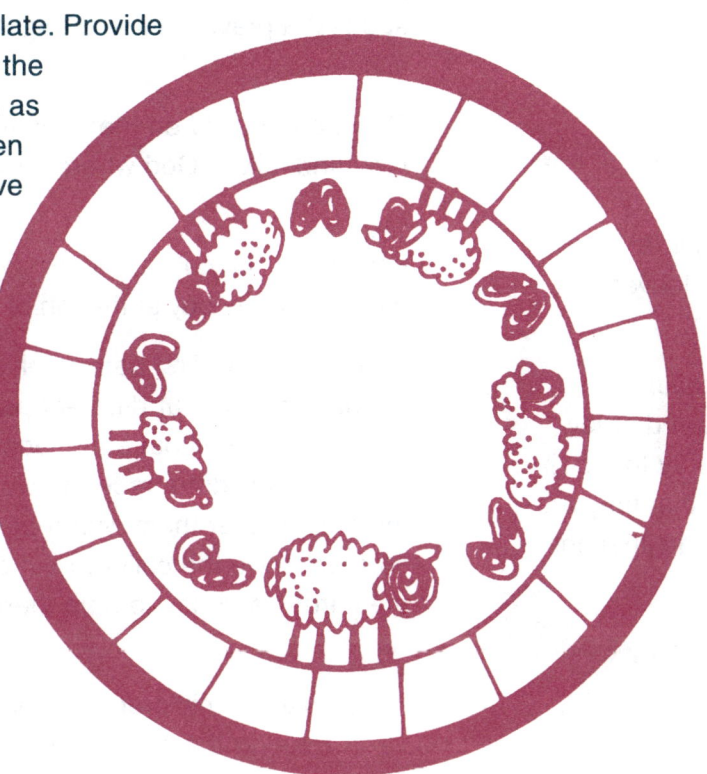

Materials for Part 2:
- *Activity Page 108*
- scissors

Talking to God (Part 2)

Theme: We can talk to God.

Purpose:
• *to help the children understand that when we talk and listen to God we are praying.*

Beginning

As the children enter the room, have Sudie Squirrel welcome them. Then help the children find the leaves with their names on them and place them on the tree.

Gather the children in a circle on the floor. Ask the children whether they ever pray to God all by themselves. What do they say to God? Do they listen to God? Where do they pray to God? Explain that you are going to act something out and that they are to guess what you are doing. Pantomime the following situations using exaggerated motions without speaking:

- eating a meal
- playing ball
- sleeping
- riding a bike
- taking a walk.

When the children have guessed the situations, tell them that no matter what time of day it is or what we are doing, we can always talk to God and tell God whatever is in our hearts. Pantomime eating a meal again, but this time, before you begin to "eat," fold your hands, bow your head, and pray silently for a minute or two. Then ask whether the children can guess what you might have said to God in your heart before you began to eat. (*Thank you, God, for this good food.*) Re-do each of the pantomimes and have the children suggest a prayer that you might be saying to God in each situation.

Remind the children that God is everywhere, which means we can pray and talk to God wherever we are.

Middle

Pass out a copy of *Activity Page 108* to each child. Call the children's attention to the boy at the top of the page. What is he doing?

Read aloud the first paragraph on the page. Draw the children's attention to the four different prayer cards. Read each one of them aloud. Then spell out each letter of the word that needs to be filled in. Let the children trace the words with their fingers first. Then let them trace over them with a pencil, crayon, or marker. When finished, have the children cut out their cards. Suggest they use the cards each day to help them remember to pray to God.

End

Take the children on a prayer hunt. Walk with the children through the building. Visit various places such as the cafeteria, the playground, the church, the library, and so on. As you stop in each location, ask the children whether they can talk to God in this place. Then stop and say a prayer such as, "Jesus, we know you are with us here. Keep us safe on the playground." Continue until you work your way back to the room.

Gather the children around the prayer table. Lead them in saying one of the prayers found on *Activity Page 108.*

Extra! Extra!

 Seeds of Prayer

Give each child a large dried seed or bean. Explain that this seed or bean is to remind them to pray. Copy the following poem on a piece of tagboard for each child. Let the children decorate the tagboard using markers and stamps.

Prayer Seed

I'm your little prayer seed.
A new life from me can grow.
If you should plant and care for me,
My beauty you will know.

But as your little prayer seed,
This is what I'll do.
When you see me, talk to Jesus,
And Jesus will talk to you.

I am your little prayer seed.
I'm here to help you grow
As a friend of Jesus.
Then to others, love you'll show.

 Materials for Part 3:
- *Read to Me Page 109*
- large piece of construction paper
- red stamp pad
- construction paper for each child
- stickers

Talking to God (Part 3)

Theme: We can tell God what is in our hearts.

Purpose:
• *to help the children develop a prayerful relationship with God.*

Beginning
 As the children enter the room, have Sudie Squirrel welcome them. Then help the children find the leaves with their names on them and place them on the tree.

Gather the children in a circle on the floor. Remind the children that we have been talking about praying to God. When we pray to God, we are just talking to him. Tell the children that we are going to write a group prayer to put at our prayer table. Ask the children to think about what they would like to say to God. Encourage all the children to contribute something to be included in the prayer.

When complete, write the prayer on a large piece of construction paper and let each child make a thumbprint heart around the edge of the paper by dipping his or her thumb in a red stamp pad and placing two prints overlapping to form a heart. Place this prayer on the prayer table.

Middle
Pass out a copy of *Read to Me Page 109* to each child. Explain to the children that this is a poem about praying. It tells about different ways we can pray to God.

Read aloud each verse of the poem. When finished, point out that the first verse shows how to thank God. The second verse shows how we should ask God for help. The third verse tells God we are sorry. The fourth verse tells God we love him.

Discuss the questions at the end of the poem. Invite the children to tell you what they think is happening in each one of the illustrations around the page.

End
Gather the children in a circle and teach them the following song:

We Pray to God *(To the tune of "Mary Had a Little Lamb")*

Thank you, thank you, thank you, God;
Thank you, God; thank you, God.
Thank you, God, we pray each day.
Thank you, God, we pray.

We love you, love you, love you, God;
Love you, God; love you, God.
How wonderful you are, dear God.
We love you more each day.

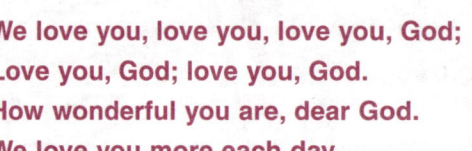

Make a copy of the group prayer on construction paper for each child. Have the children decorate a border around the prayer using various stickers. Write the date on the page. Add these pages to the children's scrapbooks.

Gather the children around the prayer table and lead them in saying the group prayer.

182

Extra! Extra!

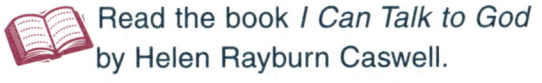 Read the book *I Can Talk to God* by Helen Rayburn Caswell.

Video Venture

Show the video *The Adventures of Prayer Bear: How to Pray,* hosted by Steve Green, produced by Sparrow Communications.

Materials for Lesson 28, Part 1:
- *Activity Page 111*
- large poster
- paper towel spools
- popsicle sticks
- Bible, candle, altar, lectern cut from construction paper
- milk caps
- crinkled shredded paper

Celebrating in Our Parish Family

Theme: We celebrate with our parish family in our churches.

Purpose:
• *to encourage awareness that we all have a part in celebrating with others in our parish.*

Beginning
As the children enter the room, have Sudie Squirrel welcome them. Then help the children find the leaves with their names on them and place them on the tree.

Gather the children in a circle or group. Tell the children that our room is very special. Take the children over to the prayer table. Ask the children what we do here. (*Talk to Jesus.*) Ask whether the children know why we have a candle on the prayer table. (*When we light the candle, it reminds us that Jesus is with us.*) Show the children the Bible and ask whether they remember the name of this special book. Remind them that this book has stories about Jesus. Then take the children to a table in the room. Ask them what we do at the table. Lead them to the conclusion that we often eat at the table. Explain that we see these same things at Mass in church.

Middle
Pass out a copy of *Activity Page 111* to each child. Call the children's attention to the picture at the top of the page. Ask where the people are going. With whom are they going? Discuss.

Read the message at the top of the page. Then draw the children's attention to the inside view of the church. Have they seen any of the objects at the bottom of the page? Discuss each one of them beginning with the altar. Comment that the prayer table we have in the room reminds us of the altar. Have the children cut out each one of the objects and paste them inside the church's interior.

End
On a large poster make the outline of a church. Use empty paper towel spools to make the walls and roof. Use popsicle sticks to make a cross at the top of the church. Have a Bible, a candle, an altar, and a lectern cut from construction paper. Invite several the children to come and glue these to the poster. Then make several pews by gluing popsicle sticks in rows in the church. Invite all the children to add their heads by gluing a milk cap right above the popsicle sticks. Have the children add hair to the heads by gluing crinkled shredded paper to the milk caps.

Gather the children around the prayer table and lead them in the following prayer: "Dear God, thank you for your gifts to us. Please help us to celebrate together at Mass. Amen."

Extra! Extra!

My Own Little Church I

Help the children make miniature church furnishings. Give each child a shoe box. Have them paint this white. Tell the children that this will be the altar. Provide a piece of white cloth for an altar cloth and show the children how to drape this over their "altars." Explain to the children that we will make other things that they see in church, only smaller versions of them. Tell the children that all the things we make can be stored in the box, and they can take them out to play with at home.

Materials for Part 2:
- *Activity Page 112*
- construction paper
- black stamp pad, marker
- tan-colored craft foam
- gray craft foam
- popsicle sticks

Celebrating in Our Parish Family (Part 2)

Theme: We celebrate the Mass with our parish community.

Purpose:

• *to help the children appreciate that when our parish community comes together to celebrate and worship God at Mass, we all can participate.*

Beginning

 As the children enter the room, have Sudie Squirrel welcome them. Then help the children find the leaves with their names on them and place them on the tree.

Gather the children in a circle on the floor. Ask the children to think about the times they have been with their families to Mass. Invite the children to tell you what we do at Mass. Remind the children that at Mass we celebrate all God's gifts to us. We say thank you to God.

Teach the children the following song:

We Celebrate the Mass
(To the tune of "Three Blind Mice")

Celebrate! Celebrate!
Come to the Mass!
Come to the Mass!
We pray, we listen, give thanks to God
For all of the gifts he has giv'n to us,
Especially Jesus, the Son of God.
Come celebrate! Celebrate!

Middle

Pass out a copy of *Activity Page 112* to each child. Read aloud the message at the top of the page. Point out the illustrations on the side of the page. Ask the children whether they have seen people do any of these activities in church. Explain that the people in the illustrations are praising and honoring God by what they do. Have the children cut out the things we do and glue them in the correct places on the page.

End

Make a Mass page for the children's scrapbooks. Help the children fold a piece of construction paper into fourths, then unfold. In the first section, write *We sing,* and have the children make black fingerprints by dipping their fingers in a stamp pad. Use a marker to turn these fingerprints into notes.

In the second section, write *We give gifts.* Give each child a piece of tan-colored craft foam. Help the children cut out an oval for bread. Draw a cup on gray craft foam for each child and have the children cut these out and glue these on this section.

In the third section, write *We listen.* Give each child two popsicle sticks to glue across the section to make pews. Have the children add heads of people in the pews by dipping their thumbs in a stamp pad and making thumbprints above the popsicle sticks.

In the fourth section, write *We pray.*

Invite the children to bow their heads now and say a prayer: "Thank you, God, for our parish family and our parish church. Amen."

Extra! Extra!

My Own Little Church II

Help the children make miniature Bibles for their churches. Give each child an empty match box. Have the children paint these with black paint. When dry, help them paint around three sides with gold or white paint. Using the gold or white paint, have the children paint a cross on the top of their match boxes. Allow to dry thoroughly. Have the children store these in their "altar boxes."

Materials for Part 3:
● *Read to Me Page 113*

Celebrating in Our Parish Family (Part 3)

Theme: With our parish family, we take part in the Mass.

Purpose:
• *to encourage appreciation for the way our community participates in the Mass.*

Beginning

As the children enter the room, have Sudie Squirrel welcome them. Then help the children find the leaves with their names on them and place them on the tree.

Take the children to the church. Walk around and find all the things that have been talked about. Then have the children sit in a pew. Sing with the children "We Celebrate the Mass" found on page 186. Then have the children kneel down and offer a prayer.

Middle

Pass out a copy of *Read to Me Page 113* to each child. Call attention to the title, "We Celebrate the Mass." Use the illustrations to show how everybody takes part in the Mass. Then read aloud the captions next to the illustrations. Ask the children what they remember best at Mass. Do they join in the singing? Do they listen to the Bible stories?

End

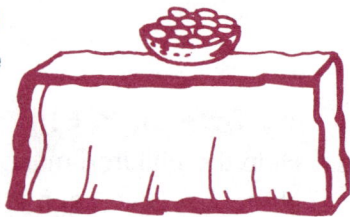

Gather the children in a group. Tell them that we will pray together the way we pray together at Mass with our parish. Explain to the children that their response to each prayer is: *Jesus, Good Shepherd, hear us.*

Leader: We join together today in praise and thanks to God for all he has given us. We pray for the whole Church throughout the world, especially our pope, our bishops, and our priests. (*Response.*)

Leader: We pray for all the people in our parish, especially our priest(s), our sisters, our teachers, and all who help in our parish. (*Response.*)

Leader: We pray for all people all over the world, especially those who are sick or hungry or in need. (*Response.*)

Leader: We pray for all those who are ill in our parish. (*Response.*)

Leader: We pray for our parents, our grandparents, our aunts and uncles, our cousins, our brothers and sisters, and all our families. (*Response.*)

Leader: We pray for our kindergarten group right here in this room together! (*Response.*)

Leader: (*Ask the children whether they know of others who need our prayers. Give them time to mention names. Then conclude.*) Thank you, Jesus, Good Shepherd, for hearing our prayer. We want to follow you always. Amen.

Extra! Extra!

My Own Little Church III

Help the children make processional crosses for their miniature churches. Explain that this cross is a cross on a long stick that is carried up to the altar at the beginning of Mass. Give each child a brown pipe cleaner and show how to form it into a cross. Then help attach this to a lollipop stick. Have the children store these in their "altar boxes."

Have the children make candle holders from air-dry clay for their "altars." Give each child two white birthday candles and a small amount of air-dry clay. Have the children press some clay around the bottom of the candles. Then have the children press the candles with clay on the table to flatten the bottom and allow the candles to stand up. Have the children put these candles in their "altar boxes." Encourage the children to bring their boxes home and play with them, setting up their "altars" like in church.

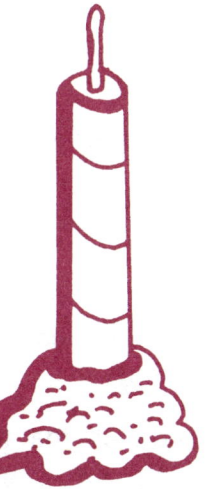
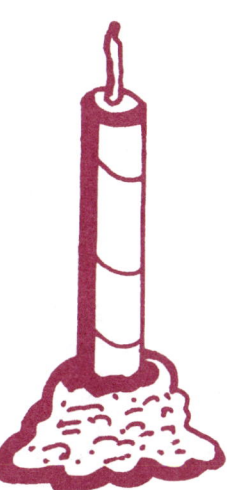

Materials for Lesson 29, Part 1:
- *Activity Page 115*
- globe
- large brown paper bag for each child
- sticky-backed velcro
- buckle shapes cut from craft foam
- two straps for each child cut from craft foam
- stickers and markers

Theme: We get ready for summer fun.

Purpose:
• *to help the children anticipate the delights to be experienced in the summertime.*

Beginning

As the children enter the room, have Sudie Squirrel welcome them. Then help the children find the leaves with their names on them and place them on the tree.

Gather the children in a circle on the floor. Remind them that there are four seasons in a year: fall, winter, spring, and summer. Tell the children that soon it will be summer. Explain that summer is an exciting, more relaxed time. Tell the children that this summer, Sudie is planning to go to camp, visit her grandmother, play baseball, go swimming, and go camping. Ask the children what they are planning to do this summer. Go around the circle and let each child have a turn to share.

Middle

Pass out a copy of *Activity Page 115* to each child. Draw the children's attention to the picture of the children at the top of the page. Ask the children whether they know what these children are doing. Why does this make us think of summer?

Read aloud the words at the top of the page. Give the children time to locate and color the hidden pictures of all the things they can do this summer. Then remind them that God is always with us, summer, fall, winter, and spring. Even though we may be doing different things and going to different places, God is everywhere, always.

End

Gather the children in a circle and show them a globe. Tell the children that we may go all over the world (spin the globe), but we want to always remember what we learned about God this year. Wherever we go, we want to take along some special reminders. Explain to the children that we will make a special knapsack to keep these things in.

 Give each child a large brown paper bag. On one large side and the two smaller sides, help the children cut away half of the bag. On the other large side (back of the bag) have the children cut to form an upside down "V" extending to the top of the bag. Have the children fold this "V" over the opening to "close" the knapsack. Put sticky-backed velcro pieces on the inside top of the "V" and on the part of the bag it touches to close. Give each child a buckle shape cut from craft foam and have them glue this on the outside of the "V." Give the children two straps made from craft foam and have them attach these to the back of the knapsack. Let the children decorate their knapsacks using stickers and markers. Keep these at kindergarten to be filled in Part 2 of this lesson.

Gather the children around the prayer table and lead them in the following prayer: "Dear God, thank you for loving us and caring for us. Thank you for being with us always. Amen."

Extra! Extra!

Good Old Summertime

Go outside and let the children enjoy some summertime activities. Bring a baseball, glove, and picnic gear outside. Let the children play pitch-and-catch. Spread out a blanket and have a picnic. Provide light snacks and popsicles for the children to enjoy.

Materials for Part 2:
- *Activity Page 116*
- toilet paper spools
- aluminum foil
- brown construction paper
- small birthday candles
- construction paper, dot stickers
- red or pink pipe cleaners

Remembering God (Part 2)

Theme: We know that God will be with us always.

Purpose:
• *to help the children discover how many wonderful things they know about God's great love for them.*

Beginning

As the children enter the room, have Sudie Squirrel welcome them. Then help the children find the leaves with their names on them and place them on the tree.

Make "microphones" with the children. Give each child an empty toilet paper spool and some foil. Have the children ball up the foil and insert it into one end of the spool. The foil ball should sit on the spool extending into the spool half way. Add more foil if needed to secure the foil ball into the spool.

Have a song festival with the children. Review and sing several of the songs learned throughout the year. Let the children use their microphones that they made.

Middle

Pass out a copy of *Activity Page 116* to each child. Read aloud the message at the top of the page. Draw the children's attention to the cross at the top of the page. Read the words under the cross. Then have the children look at the other pictures on the page. Each is a reminder of a previous lesson. Discuss one picture at a time. Encourage the children to comment about each picture and to recall what they learned.

End

Tell the children that we will put some things in our knapsacks to remind us of what we learned this year. Give each child a piece of brown construction paper. Help the children draw a cross and cut it out. Have the children put the crosses in their knapsacks as reminders that, wherever they go, God is with them.

Give each child a small birthday candle to put in the knapsacks. Tell the children this is to remind them that they should always bring the light of Jesus to everyone they meet.

Give each child a strip of construction paper and some dot stickers. Have the children put one dot sticker for each member of their family on the piece of construction paper. Tell them this is to remind them of all the things we learned about our families this year.

Give each child a red or pink pipe cleaner. Have the children shape this into a heart. This is to remind the children of all the people who love us. Have the children add these two items to their knapsacks. Encourage the children to bring their knapsacks home and share with their families all the things they have learned this year.

Gather the children around the prayer table and lead them in the following prayer: "Thank you, God, for a wonderful year in kindergarten. We look forward to our summer months because we know that you are always with us. We want to be with you forever. Amen."

Extra! Extra!

 ## Microphone Cones

Make edible microphones with the children. Give each child a flat-bottomed ice cream cone. Put a scoop of ice cream in each cone. Let the children add chocolate candy sprinkles to the ice cream. Sing one quick song using the cone as a microphone. Then eat and enjoy!

Note: Be aware of any children with food allergies before using this activity.

Live on Tape

Make a video or an audio recording of the children enjoying their song festival. Let the children watch or listen to the recording, singing along with themselves. If possible, make copies available for the children to take home and share with their families.

 ### Materials for Part 3:

- *Read to Me Page 117*
- children's year-end scrapbooks
- craft materials, markers, stamps, stickers
- circles cut from craft foam
- green paint
- sticky magnets
- pitcher
- lemons, sugar, water, ice
- paper cups

Remembering God
(Part 3)

Theme: We can be aware of God in the summer and all the time.

Purpose:
• to encourage the children to be aware of God's presence and to respond to God's love during the summer.

Beginning
Ahead of time, put together the children's scrapbooks from the pages that have been saved all year long. Attach a blank piece of construction paper for the cover.

As the children enter the room, have Sudie Squirrel welcome them. Then help the children find the leaves with their names on them and place them on the tree.

Gather the children in a circle on the floor. Show the children one of the scrapbooks. Flip through the pages, one at a time, and review all the wonderful things that they have done and learned this past year.

Middle
Pass out a copy of *Read to Me Page 117* to each child. Draw the children's attention to the illustrations. Tell them this is a picture story about the Barry family taking a trip. Invite the children to use the pictures to say what the family will do. Invite the children to imagine that we are going along on this family trip. Ask the children how the Barry family will show they love God while on the trip.

After the children have discussed the picture story, invite them to tell how they plan to show their love for God during the summer. Who will help them? What will they do?

End

Set up three centers and move around them with the children. In the first center, provide various craft materials, markers, stamps, and stickers. Give each child his or her scrapbook. Have the children decorate the cover using the materials provided.

In the second center, provide circles cut from craft foam for each child. Have the children add green paint for land to make a globe. Attach a piece of sticky magnet to the back. Tell the children to put this on their refrigerators to remind them that God is with them wherever they go.

In the third center make a cool and refreshing summertime drink, lemonade. Provide several lemons, cut in half. Help the children squeeze them into a pitcher. Add sugar, water, ice, and stir. Give each child a cup of lemonade to enjoy.

To conclude this year, take down all the summer decorations around the room. Give the children the summer leaves with their names on them to take home. Let the children take home their scrapbooks and their Bible story booklets.

Gather the children around the prayer table and lead them in the following prayer: "Dear God, it is wonderful to know you are everywhere. We know you will hear us when we pray to you. Thank you, God, for loving us and caring for us. Amen."

Extra! Extra!

The Year-End Scrapbook

Take a picture of each child with Sudie Squirrel. Mount this picture on a piece of construction paper and write the words *See how I've grown* on the bottom. Add this as the last page in the children's scrapbooks.

Read the book *The Best Vacation Ever* by Stuart J. Murphy. Let the children share stories of their vacations. Ask the children whether any of them will be traveling this summer. Suggest that they each take a vacation in their own backyards like in the story.

See how I've grown.

Materials for Lesson 30, Part 1:
- *Activity Pages 119 and 120*
- various craft supplies
- aluminum pie pans
- newspaper or cardboard
- dull pencils
- golf tees
- paint pen
- tissue paper

Theme: Our mothers bring us into life.

Purpose:
• *to develop an awareness in the children of the need to thank our mothers and those who love and care for us as mothers do.*

Beginning

As the children enter the room, have Sudie Squirrel welcome them. Then help the children find the leaves with their names on them and place them on the tree.

Gather the children in a circle on the floor. Remind the children that God gives us our families to love and care for us. Tell the children that our mothers do special things for us and show us how much God loves us. Go around the circle and let each child tell the ways his or her mother shows love to him or her.

Explain to the children that a special day is set aside each year to honor mothers and those who love and care for us like mothers. We say "thank you" to our mothers on this special day. Point out to the children that although we say "thank you" in a special way on Mother's Day, our mothers deserve our love, respect, and help all year long.

Teach the children the following song:

Mom *(To the tune of "Three Blind Mice")*

I love my mom.	She's the nicest mom that I know.
I love my mom.	She takes care of me, wherever we go.
She loves me too.	She helps me learn and she helps me to grow.
She loves me too.	She's my mom!

Middle

Pass out a copy of *Activity Page 119* to each child. Call the children's attention to the picture at the top of the page. Ask the children how they know that these two people love each other.

Read aloud the words on the top of the page. Point out that one of the ways we can say thank you on Mother's Day is to give our mothers a special card. Encourage the children to use various craft supplies to create something beautiful on the left-hand side of the card.

Have the children turn the page over to look at *Activity Page 120.* Read aloud the message at the top of the page. Ask the children to draw their mothers or the person who takes care of them on the card. Encourage them to print their own names. You may want to go around and print the other person's name under the greeting on each child's card. Have the children cut out the cards and fold where indicated. Encourage the children to give the card with a hug and kiss on Mother's Day.

End

To make a gift for their moms, provide each child with an aluminum pie pan. Working on a layer of newspaper or cardboard, help them trace their hands, using a dull pencil, on the bottom of the pans. Give each child a golf tee and show them how to punch tiny holes along the pencil mark. Using a paint pen, write the child's name and the date on each one. Let the children bring these home for their mothers on Mother's Day.

Gather the children around the prayer table and lead them in the prayer found on *Activity Page 120.*

Extra! Extra!

 Share any of the following books with the children:

I Love You, Little One, written by Nancy Tafuri, published by Scholastic, Inc. (New York) 1998.

If I Were Your Mother, written by Margaret Park Bridges, published by Morrow Junior Books (New York) 1999.

Ask Mr. Bear, written by Marjorie Flack, published by Live Oak Media (Pine Plains, NY) 1991.

The Mother's Day Mice, written by Eve Bunting, published by Houghton Mifflin Company (Boston) 1988.

Mama, Do You Love Me?, written by Barbara M. Joosse, published by Chronicle Books (San Francisco, CA) 1991.

Monster Mama, written by Liz Rosenberg, published by Putnam Publishing Group (New York) 1997.

What Mommies Do Best, written by Laura Numeroff, published by Simon & Schuster Children's Publishing (New York) 1998.

A Present for Mama Bear, written by Bonnie Staenberg, published by Scholastic, Inc. (New York) 1999.

Mama Zooms, written by Jane Cowen-Fletcher, published by Scholastic, Inc. (New York) 1996.

Jonathan and His Mommy, written by Irene Smalls, published by Little Brown & Company (New York) 1994.

Materials for Part 2:
- *Activity Pages 121 and 122*
- empty baby food jars with lids
- salt
- food coloring
- rubbing alcohol
- zippered plastic bags
- tissue paper

Father's Day (Part 2)

Theme: Fathers love and care for us and help bring us God's gift of life.

Purpose:
- *to affirm the role of fathers in bringing us God's gifts.*

Beginning

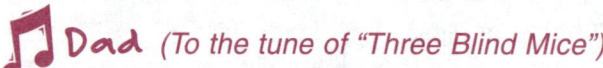As the children enter the room, have Sudie Squirrel welcome them. Then help the children find the leaves with their names on them and place them on the tree.

Gather the children in a circle. Remind them that we belong to our families and that God gives us our families to love and care for us. Tell the children that our fathers do special things for us and show us how much God loves us. Go around the circle and let each child tell the ways his or her father shows love to him or her.

Explain to the children that Father's Day will be coming during the summer. It is a day set aside to honor our fathers for all the love and care they give us all year round.

Teach the children the following song:

♪ **Dad** *(To the tune of "Three Blind Mice")*

I love my dad. I love my dad.
He loves me, too. He loves me, too.
He's the nicest man that I know.
He takes care of me, wherever we go.
He helps me learn and he helps me to grow.
He's my dad!

Middle

Pass out a copy of *Activity Page 121* to each child. Remind the children that God loves and cares for us through our fathers and those that care for us like fathers. Call attention to the picture of the girl giving her father a big hug. Tell the children that this is a very nice way a child can say "thank you" to a father who does so much for his family. Read aloud the message at the top of the page. Ask the children what gift they would like to give on Father's Day. Then invite the children to draw it on the card.

Have the children turn their pages over to *Activity Page 122.* Read the message at the top of the page. Encourage the children to talk about the person who brings them God's love and care. Help the children write the word *Dad* on the left side of the card and their names on the right side of the card. Then have the children cut out the card and fold. Remind the children to save the card and give it with a big hug to their dads on Father's Day.

End

Help the children make paperweights for their dads. Provide each child with an empty baby food jar. Make colored salt by putting salt in a zippered plastic bag. Add a few drops of food coloring and a teaspoon of rubbing alcohol. Close the bag securely and shake until the color is evenly distributed. Pour into a bowl to dry. Make several different colors. Show the children how to add the colored salt to their jars in layers of different colors. Have the children fill the jars, then attach the lids securely. Help the children wrap the paperweights in tissue paper.

Gather the children around the prayer table and lead them in the prayer found on *Activity Page 122.*

Extra! Extra!

 Share any of the following books with the children:

I Love My Daddy Because . . ., written by Laurel Potter-Gaylord, published by Putnam Publishing Group (New York) 1991.

Daddy and Me, written by Catherine Daly-Weir, published by Penguin Putnam Books for Young Readers (New York) 1999.

Daddy Will Be There, written by Lois G. Grambling, published by Greenwillow Books (New York) 1998.

What Daddies Do Best, written by Laura Numeroff, published by Simon & Schuster Children's Publishing (New York) 1998.

A Perfect Father's Day, written by Eve Bunting, published by Houghton Mifflin (Boston) 1993.

Papa, Please Get the Moon for Me, written by Eric Carle, published by Simon & Schuster Children's Publishing (New York) 1991.

Just Like My Dad, written by Tricia Gardella, published by HarperCollins Children's Books (New York) 1996.

A Special Kind of Love, written by Stephen Michael King, published by Scholastic, Inc. (New York) 1996.

Materials for Lesson 31:
- *Activity Pages 123 and 124*
- children's Bible
- Sadlier's *Bible Felt Art Kit*

Mary Is Our Mother

Theme: We learn to ask Mary to help us.

Purpose:

• *to encourage the children to pray to Mary, our mother.*

Beginning

As the children enter the room, have Sudie Squirrel welcome them. Then help the children find the leaves with their names on them and place them on the tree.

Gather the children in a circle on the floor. Remind the children that Mary is in heaven with God. Stress to the children that they can talk to Mary and pray to her. Mary can ask Jesus to listen to our prayers. Jesus loves Mary, his mother, so much that he listens very carefully to what she asks him to do. Remind the children of the story of the wedding at Cana.

Middle

Pass out a copy of *Activity Page 123* to each child. Call the children's attention to the family group at the top of the page. Ask the children who they think the people are.

Now have the children look at the portrait of Mary on their page. Read aloud the message about the picture. Discuss why and how Mary said yes to God. When we trust someone, we do what that person asks. Ask the children why they think Mary did what God asked. Remind them that this great event, the birth of Jesus, happened on Christmas Day. Ask the children to tell you who came to see Jesus when he was born. Ask the children what they themselves might have said to Mary on the night of Jesus' birth.

Have the children turn their pages over to *Activity Page 124*. Read aloud the message at the top of the page. Ask the children to tell you when they can pray to Mary. In church? At night in your home? In the room? Tell the children that they can pray to Mary anytime, any place. Mary will hear their prayers. Have the children cut out the picture of Mary. Tell them to take it home so it will help them remember to pray to her.

End

Gather the children. Tell them that God asked Mary to be Jesus' mother. Mary said yes to God. We know this because there is a story in the Bible that tells all about this. Read from a children's Bible or tell in your own words Luke 1:26–38. If available, use Sadlier's *Bible Felt Art Kit* to enhance the story. Let the children act out the story.

Teach the children the following song:

♪ **Mary, Our Mother** *(To the tune of "Away in a Manger")*

Hail Mary, our mother.
Hail Jesus, your son.
You know us and love us.
You care for each one!

We pray to you, Mary,
To help us each day.
Will you tell dear Jesus
To you both we'll pray?

Gather the children around the prayer table and lead them in saying the "Hail Mary." (Explain to the children that "Hail, Mary" is the same as saying "Hello, Mary.")

Extra! Extra!

Bring Flowers of the Fairest

Go to church and show the children the statue of Mary. Give each child a fresh flower. Have the children present these flowers to Mary while singing the song "Mary, Our Mother" found on page 200.

Materials for Lesson 32:
- *Activity Pages 125 and 126*
- balloon drawn on colorful construction paper for each child
- string or ribbon
- bows cut from construction paper
- markers, glue
- cupcakes, icing, candy sprinkles

Theme: Every birthday reminds us of God's gift of love.

Purpose:

• *to help the children be aware that on our birthdays we celebrate God's gift of life.*

Beginning

As the children enter the room, have Sudie Squirrel welcome them. Then help the children find the leaves with their names on them and place them on the tree.

Gather the children in a circle. Explain to the children that we celebrate the day they were born because this is the day that God gave them to us. This is a very special day.

Make a birthday graph with the children. Give each child a balloon drawn on a piece of colorful construction paper. Have the children write their names on the balloons and cut them out. Tape a piece of string or ribbon to the bottom of each balloon. Gather all the balloons of the children who have birthdays in January and attach these in a bunch to the room wall or a bulletin board. Attach a bow cut from construction paper. Write on the bow the word January. Continue in this way for each of the other eleven months.

Middle

Pass out a copy of *Activity Page 125* to each child. Ask the children to pretend it is everybody's birthday today. Sing "Happy Birthday" to all the children. Invite the children to decorate their cakes with markers. Then have the children cut out the candles and glue on as many candles as needed. Help as needed.

Have the children turn their pages over to *Activity Page 126.* Call the children's attention to the picture of the child on the top of the page. Ask the children whether they know what he is doing. Is it fun? Read the lines at the top of the page. Invite the children to draw some special things that they will do on their birthday inside the frame. Then have them cut out the frame (the cake is on the other side) and bring it home.

End

Have a birthday celebration. Give each child a cupcake. Help them spread icing on the cupcake and decorate with candy sprinkles. Put a candle in each child's cupcake. Sing "Happy Birthday" and let the children pretend to blow out the candles. Let the children enjoy their cupcakes.

Gather the children around the prayer table and lead them in the prayer found on *Activity Page 126.*

Extra! Extra!

🧴 Looking Ahead

Give each child an empty margarine tub. Carefully cut slits in the shape of "X"s in the bottom of the tubs. Turn the margarine tubs upside down to make cakes. Invite the children to decorate their "cakes" using glitter glue, rickrack, and other art materials. Have the children insert in the slits the number of candles needed on their cakes on their next birthday.

🎵 A Birthday Song

(To the tune of "London Bridge")

You're a special gift of God,
Gift of God, gift of God.
You're a special gift of God.
Happy Birthday!

Notes